CROSSCURRENTS OF CULTURE

ARTS OF AFRICA AND THE AMERICAS IN ALABAMA COLLECTIONS

CROSSCURRENTS OF CULTURE

ARTS OF AFRICA AND THE AMERICAS IN ALABAMA COLLECTIONS

Manuel Jordán

Mary Villadsen

BIRMINGHAM MUSEUM OF ART

BIRMINGHAM, ALABAMA

Crosscurrents of Culture:
Art of Africa and the Americas in Alabama Collections
May 18–August 31, 1997
Birmingham Museum of Art
Birmingham, Alabama

© 1997 Birmingham Museum of Art
Birmingham, Alabama

Printed in the United States of America
All rights reserved

This catalogue was designed by Joan K. Kennedy with photography by Harold and Brent Kilgore. It was printed by Craftsman Printing, Inc., on Zanders Mega Dull 100 lb. text and 111 lb. cover with a gloss varnish.

Library of Congress Cataloging-in-Publication Data
Jordán, Manuel
        Crosscurrents of culture : arts of Africa and the Americas in
Alabama collections / Manuel Jordán, Mary Villadsen.
            p.   cm.
        Catalog of an exhibition held at the Birmingham Museum of Art, May
18–Aug. 31, 1997.
        Includes bibliographical references.
        ISBN 0-931394-42-2   (softcover : alk. paper)
            1. Indian art—Exhibitions. 2. Art, African—Exhibitions.
3. Indians—Material culture—Exhibitions. 4. Material culture—
Africa—Exhibitions. 5. America—Antiquities—Exhibitions.
6. Africa—Antiquities—Exhibitions.   I. Villadsen, Mary.
II. Birmingham Museum of Art (Birmingham, Ala.)   III. Title.
E59.A7J67   1997
708.161—dc21   97-15403
                                                                              CIP

ISBN 0-931394-42-2

Cover, front, left to right: Ceramic mask; Colima culture, West Mexico; fired clay and slip; collection of Charlotte and Brent Springford. Engraved "Weeping-Eye" mask; Late Mississippian period, Nodena phase (1400–1650); Nodena culture, Mississippi County, Arkansas; shell; collection of the University of Alabama Museums, Office of Archaeological Services, Moundville. Female mask; 1900–1925; Songye people, Zaire; wood, raffia, and pigments; Birmingham Museum of Art purchase with funds provided by June and J. Mason Davis, Mr. and Mrs. Edward M. Friend, Fred and Ellen Elsas, the Committee for Traditional Arts, the Traditional Arts Acquisition Fund, and the General Acquisitions Fund. **Cover, back:** Man's coat; collected in 1843; Metis style, eastern Dakotas; leather, porcupine quills, dyes, and glass beads; the collection of the Alabama Department of Archives and History, Montgomery. Cylinder vessel with catfish; 600–800; Maya culture, Guatemala; fired clay and slip; collection of Randolph O. George. Female nail figure; Vili people (?), Republic of Congo/Zaire; wood, metal, fibers, animal skull, and pigments; Birmingham Museum of Art purchase with funds provided by the Junior Patrons, the Committee for Traditional Arts, Mrs. Bernard S. Steiner, and Museum visitors.
Frontispiece, top: *Quetzalcóatl*; 1200–1519; Aztec culture, Central Mexico; stone and pigment; Birmingham Museum of Art purchase with funds provided by Dr. and Mrs. Keith Merrill, Jr.; Mr. and Mrs. F. Dixon Brooke, Jr.; the bequest of Mrs. G. F. McDonnell; Mrs. Margaret Steeves; Mr. and Mrs. Charles Grisham; Mr. and Mrs. Hugh Jacks; the Hess Endowed Fund; and the Acquisition Fund. **Center:** Storage vessel; 1890–1900; Zuni people, New Mexico; fired clay and slip; collection of Dick Jemison. **Bottom:** Male mask; Songye people, Zaire; wood and pigments; collection of Fred and Ellen Elsas.

CONTENTS

FOREWORD

The Birmingham Museum of Art is pleased to present *Crosscurrents of Culture: Arts of Africa and the Americas in Alabama Collections*. This exhibition brings together, for the first time, the rich and varied holdings of African, Native American, and Precolumbian art in Alabama private and public collections. The majority of these works of art, selected for their quality and cultural significance, have never been exhibited publicly before. We are extremely grateful to the public institutions but are especially indebted to the private collectors who have so generously shared not only these remarkable objects but also their knowledge and research gathered from years of collecting. This exhibition is a tribute to their passion for collecting objects of outstanding quality and for their understanding of the importance of sharing this knowledge with a broader audience.

Crosscurrents reflects the commitment of the Museum to collect and exhibit in these areas and I would like to take this opportunity to recognize the efforts of the Museum's first director, Richard Foster Howard, for his understanding of the importance of Native American and Precolumbian art. The Museum's purchase in 1956 of the Rasmussen Collection of Northwest Coast material, just five years after the Museum was founded, forms the basis of our Native American collection. Mr. Howard was instrumental in developing an appreciation for Precolumbian art in the community, which encouraged acquisitions in that area as well. The first curator of this collection, Ellen Friend Elsas, brought a depth of scholarship coupled with a commitment to build partnerships between the Museum and the greater community. We are indebted to her for her vision and dedication in beginning, and then building, our collection of African art and for working to create related educational programs. In addition, many individuals have been instrumental in helping fund the Museum's acquisitions and programs in African, Precolumbian, and Native American art. Key to this effort is the Committee for the Traditional Arts, and I would like to especially thank members June Davis, Randy Gray, Elias Hendricks, Dr. Grady Nunn, Dr. Charles Ochs, and Dr. Dannetta K. Thornton Owens.

Manuel Jordán, Curator of the Arts of Africa and the Americas, is expanding on this work, and *Crosscurrents* is just one example of his ability to connect this Museum with a broader audience. Through his scholarship and discerning eye he has already had tremendous impact on the department's acquisitions and long range plans. I want to particularly commend him for his work on this exhibition and publication and to also recognize the work of Mary Villadsen, Assistant Curator. It is through their efforts that this project is a reality and that the arts of Africa and the Americas are playing an ever greater role in the cultural life of Alabama.

Gail Andrews Trechsel
R. Hugh Daniel Director

ACKNOWLEDGMENTS

Crosscurrents of Culture is the result of collaboration between the Birmingham Museum of Art, other institutions, and art collectors in the state of Alabama. We wish to express our gratitude to the many African, Precolumbian, and Native American art collectors who so kindly "opened their doors" to this project. We also wish to thank the following public and private institutions, and their staffs, for sharing their art, documents, and expertise. These include the Alabama Department of Archives and History in Montgomery; the University of Alabama Museums, Office of Archaeological Services at Moundville; the University of Alabama Museums, Alabama Museum of Natural History, Tuscaloosa; the Anniston Museum of Natural History; the Wiregrass Museum of Art in Dothan; and the Warner Collection of the Gulf States Paper Corporation. Other institutions that made their collections available to us include the Tuskegee Institute, the Baptist Women's Missionary Union, and the Mobile Art Museum.

The Birmingham Museum of Art, Department of the Arts of Africa and the Americas, also recognizes the continuous support provided by the City of Birmingham, the Museum Board, the Members of the Museum, the Alabama Humanities Foundation, the Alabama State Council on the Arts, the Committee for Traditional Arts, and the Junior Patrons of the Museum. We thank our Director, Gail Andrews Trechsel, for her encouragement and vision. Special thanks are extended to Joan Kennedy for designing this catalogue, and to Harold and Brent Kilgore for the photography. We also appreciate the efforts of the Museum staff in making the exhibition, catalogue, and events a success, in particular Development Director Holly Booyse. Ellen Friend Elsas, former Curator of the Department of the Arts of Africa and the Americas, deserves full recognition for developing the African, Precolumbian, and Native American permanent collections in the 1980s. Her knowledge and continuous support is greatly appreciated. The arts of Africa and the Americas often stress the view that a prosperous future can only be secured by acknowledging the achievements of our ancestors and predecessors. In that spirit we wish to recognize the significant contributions made to our department by Rena Hill Selfe and General Edward M. Friend, Jr. We dedicate this catalogue to them, and to other personal guardians, James A. Villadsen, Manuel Jordán López, Carmen Rabelo Rodríguez, and Mr. Chipoya.

Man's fringed shirt, collected in 1843, Upper Missouri style, possibly Blackfeet; leather, porcupine quills, dyes, and pigment; collection of the Alabama Department of Archives and History, Montgomery.

Dancing headdress frontlet, early 20th century, Tlingit people, Southeastern Alaska; wood, pigment, abalone shell, flour sack, ermine skins, flicker feathers, sea lion whiskers, and string; Birmingham Museum of Art purchase from the Rasmussen Collection.

Standing couple, early 20th century, Baule people, Ivory Coast; wood and pigment; collection of Mary E. Cumming.

Vessel in the form of a howling dog, 200 B.C.–A.D. 200, Maya culture, Guatemala, Kaminaljuyú or Pacific Coast; fired clay and slip; collection of Randolph O. George.

INTRODUCTION

Crosscurrents of Culture: Arts of Africa and the Americas in Alabama Collections celebrates the enthusiastic spirit and discerning vision of Alabama private collectors and institutions in gathering outstanding works of art representative of many of the most important art producing cultures of Africa and the Americas. African, Precolumbian, and Native American cultures have created a variety of art forms to illustrate and embody principles of cosmology, religion, philosophy, and social order. The exhibition provides the museum visitor with an opportunity to compare how diverse artistic traditions approach ideas related to birth, growth, death, regeneration, social and political order, education, history, and religion. African, Precolumbian, and Native American art represents tangible ideas and concepts applicable to all societies. The exhibition seeks to present these works of art as part of an inclusive, shared, human cultural heritage.

The catalogue is organized in three parts, beginning with African Art and followed by Native American and Precolumbian Art sections. Objects with descriptive/analytical essays in each division are arranged geographically by ethnic or culture group. Other African, Native American, and Precolumbian art objects without descriptive essays, including additional culture groups, are included at the end of each section following a similar geographical order. The African section begins with the northern Tuareg, followed by the Bidjogo of Bissagos Islands, and the West African Lobi, Dan, Baule, Yoruba, Igbo, and Ejagham. Groups of the Equatorial Forest and the Southern Savannah of Africa, including the Fang, Bembe, Vili, Yaka, Pende, Chokwe, Songye, Hemba, and Eastern Bembe, follow. Zigua and Mahafaly pieces of Tanzania and Madagascar conclude the catalogue of African objects and essays.

The Native American art section begins with the Tlingit, Haida, Nootka, and Haisla cultures of the American Northwest coastal region, continuing with the Anasazi, Mimbres, Zuni, Pueblo, Navajo, and Apache of the Southwestern United States. Pieces from the Plains

Stone head or mask, 200–750, Teotihuacan culture, Central Mexico; green stone; loan of the Birmingham Museum of Art Acquisition Fund, Inc.; gift of Mrs. Gay Barna in memory of her mother, Rose Montgomery Melhado.

Dancing robe/blanket, 1875–1900, Tlingit people, Chilkat style, Southeast Washington/British Columbia; mountain goat wool spun with yellow cedar bark, dyes; collection of Mary E. Cumming.

region include the Blackfeet and the Sioux cultures, and the Canadian Chippewa to the north. Ancient pieces from Mississippian cultures and other examples from the Southeast conclude the section on Native American Art with related essays.

The Precolumbian Art segment begins with the Colima, continuing with the Maya, Veracruz, Olmec, Teotihuacan, and Aztec cultures of Mesoamerica. The Cocle of Panama, and the Moche, Huari, and Inca cultures of ancient Peru, conclude this section.

Maps with the location of the different culture groups precede the African, Native American, and Precolumbian art divisions. Bibliographical information and other research sources of reference are included at the end of each part. We hope this will aid the reader in further studying these cultures and the form and meaning of the arts they have created.

Crosscurrents of Culture is the result of collaborative efforts between the Birmingham Museum of Art and private collectors and other museums and institutions in the state of Alabama. Workshops and public discussions, organized in conjunction with this exhibition, seek to establish a creative dialogue among institutions, collectors, scholars, art dealers, and the public regarding how best to secure objects of artistic and cultural significance for the enjoyment of future generations in Alabama. *Crosscurrents of Culture: Arts of Africa and the Americas in Alabama Collections* presents African, Precolumbian, and Native American art as part of the world's cultural heritage that Alabama preserves in the spirit of cultural diversity.

Manuel Jordán
Curator
Arts of Africa and the Americas

Dough bowl, 1910–1920, Santo Domingo Pueblo, New Mexico; fired clay and slip; Birmingham Museum of Art purchase in memory of James A. Villadsen with funds provided by family and friends, the docents and staff of the Museum, the Committee for the Traditional Arts, Martha Villadsen Wright, Mississippi Materials Company, Dunn Investment Company, and Orbital Sciences Corporation.

Cylinder vessel with seated lords, 600–800, Maya culture, Lowland region; fired clay and slip; collection of Randolph O. George.

AFRICAN CULTURES

1. Taureg
2. Bidjogo
3. Dogon
4. Peul
5. Lobi
6. Dan
7. Senufo
8. Baule
9. Akan
10. Yoruba
11. Igbo
12. Ibibio
13. Ogoni
14. Ejagham
15. Bekom
16. Mambila
17. Fang

18. Kota
19. Bembe
20. Vili
21. Yaka
22. Holo
23. Pende
24. Chokwe
25. Songye
26. Hemba
27. Bembe
    (eastern)
28. Zigua
29. Mahafaly
30. Ndeble

AFRICA

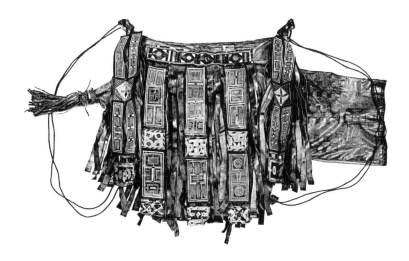

SADDLE BAG

Mid-20th century
Tuareg people, Northern Africa
Leather and pigments
29 x 56 x 5 inches
Collection of Elias Hendricks III

The majority of modern Tuareg are nomadic herders who inhabit vast regions of the Sahara and engage in the trade of salt and other goods with sub-Saharan groups in Mali, Burkina Faso, Niger, Nigeria, and Chad (Erzini 1995, 178–79). Some Tuareg artists are recognized as accomplished metalworkers (Amick 1995), who produce elaborate crosses, cosmetic boxes, locks, swords, blades, and other implements by using contrasting layers of metals—silver, copper, brass, and/or tin—in complex geometric patterns and designs (Kerr 1997). Horse and camel saddles, beds, and other objects are constructed by combining wood, metal, and leather. Tuareg also create large camel or goat leather bags that serve as containers to carry their belongings. This saddle bag shows characteristic Tuareg designs that were drawn or created by juxtaposing and contrasting bands of openwork leather in different tones and colors, both dyed and natural. Among other symbolic motifs represented on this bag, the "Tuareg cross" serves as protection against evil. The cross also refers to the four cardinal points and to different stages in the cycle of life (Kerr 1997).

STANDING FEMALE FIGURE

(Negan nu)
Early 20th century
Bidjogo people, Guinea-Bissau, Bissagos
   Archipelago, Carache Island
Wood, nail, and pigments
21 x 7 x 5¾ inches
Collection of Mary E. Cumming

Bidjogo male initiation societies are divided into four age groups called *cadene* (around six years of age), *canhocan* (around 10 years of age), *cabaro* (around puberty), and *camabi* (between twenty-five and thirty years of age) (Galhano 1971, 10–11). Different types of Bidjogo masks are assigned to specific age grades, and different forms of figurative sculpture are carved by young men of the *cabaro* society. Women choose their future husbands from those who are initiated into *cabaro*. *Cabaro* initiates carve figurative staffs that their future wives recognize when the initiates return to the village after months of initiation (Veiga de Oliveira and Dias 1972, 98–135). Although some Bidjogo masks are well known, information about their figurative sculpture is scarce. Relatively few Bidjogo carved wooden sculptures are preserved in museum or private collections. This Bidjogo figure, called *iran* or specifically *negan nu*, was made to contain the spirit of a female protective ancestor. Figures of this type may have been used in conjunction with initiations and during funerary ceremonies for high ranking members of society. Danielle Gallois Duquette (1979, 31) suggests that figurative sculptures may be carried by men or women during ceremonial dances.

This figure's robust physical appearance indicates the ancestor's good health. The hat, carved as part of the figure, accentuates the female ancestor's high social status and possibly identifies her as an *okinka* or priestess. A similar figure, from the island of Carache, is part of the permanent collection of the Overseas Museum of Ethnology in Lisbon, Portugal (Veiga de Oliveira and Dias 1972, 92).

STANDING FEMALE FIGURE

(Bateba phuwe)
Early 20th century
Lobi people, Burkina Faso
Wood and raffia string
21¹/₄ x 4³/₄ x 4 inches
Collection of Fred and Ellen Elsas

Lobi people of Burkina Faso create male and female figures called *bateba,* which they place in shrines to serve as intermediaries between supernatural spirits (*thila*) and humans. Piet Meyer's (1981) study of art and religion among the Lobi has provided significant information about the meaning of different *bateba* figure types. This figure, with a relatively relaxed posture, is within the category of "normal *bateba*" or *bateba phuwe*. The figure served to protect a Lobi family or community from misfortunes, granting fertility and success to its owners. Christopher Roy (1992, 40) has indicated that there is an ancestral spirit association to these figures. The subtle combination of naturalistic and stylized features, characteristic of this figure, reinforce the human and supernatural dualistic attributes of *bateba*.

This figure's expressive facial features suggest that the *bateba* is engaged in a state of mediation for its owners. The heavily crusted surface of this figure indicates continuous ritual use in its original context.

SPOON WITH ANTHROPOMORPHIC HEAD

(Wakemia or *mawuoshlumia)*
Early 20th century
Dan people, Liberia
Wood, metal, and pigment
25 x 5³/₄ x 6 inches
Collection of Mary E. Cumming

Large and elaborately carved wooden spoons are owned by Dan women who are recognized as the "most hospitable" or industrious in their communities. The most hospitable woman is called *wakede,* and her spoon *(wakemia)* embodies the spirit that aides the owner in her generous acts and in her success in cultivation (Fischer and Himmelheber 1984, 123–25). Spoons of this type are held by their female owners during festivals or feasts where these hospitable women are honored.

This figurative spoon, known as *mawuoshlumia* because it contains an anthropomorphic head, was created by a skilled carver with a unique sense for style. Sinuous long lines define the contours of the spirit's face, arching behind the crown to represent a simple but elegant coiffure. The elaborate rings on the figure's neck, incised body patterns, and finely conceived spoon's bowl create an image of prestige and elegance worthy of an important woman and her spiritual companion.

STANDING COUPLE

(Asie usu)
Early 20th century
Baule people, Ivory Coast
Wood and pigment
21 x 4¼ x 4¼ inches
and 16¾ x 4¼ x 4¼ inches
Collection of Mary E. Cumming

Baule couples represent *asie usu* or nature/bush spirits that may distress the lives of humans. Spiritual afflictions are manifested in different ways. Spirits may bring insanity, and sometimes unexpected supernatural abilities, to humans. Possession by nature spirits may cause a person to become a *komien* spirit medium or diviner (Ravenhill 1994, 54–56). To appease upset nature spirits, a Baule diviner may prescribe the carving of *asie usu*. The nature spirits are controlled through their "personification" as they become human figures in the hands of Baule carvers (Ravenhill, 56). Subsequent offerings made to these sculptural representations may restore harmony in the life of an afflicted individual. In the case of a diviner's *asie usu*, the figures may be displayed publicly as a evidence of a diviner's spiritual connections.

This *asie usu* couple is carved in a rather unusual style. The figures have long, slim bodies and soft contour lines that convey a subtle sense of elegance. Although the figures stand straight, the large open eyes, slightly flexed legs, gesture of the arms, and "inward" tilting of the headdresses or coiffures insinuate that the spirits are alive in their assumed human forms. These figures are stylistically related to an *asie usu* couple in The Metropolitan Museum of Art and to a single figure in a private collection (Kerchache, Paudrat and Stéphan 1988, 126–27, 386).

STAFF FOR SHANGO

(*Oshe Shango*)
Early 20th century
Yoruba people, Nigeria
Wood, glass beads, and pigment
18 x 3 x 3 inches
Collection of Fred and Ellen Elsas

This staff was used by a devotee of Shango, the Yoruba deity or *orisha* of thunder and lightning. John Pemberton III has documented different Yoruba accounts on the extent of Shango's supernatural powers (Drewal, Pemberton III, and Abiodun 1989, 157–58). In one version, Shango (the fourth king of Oyo-Ile), experimenting with his supernatural powers, accidentally caused lightning to strike his town causing death to members of his own family. Perturbed by his actions, Shango decided to commit suicide. This story implies that the abuse of power has tragic consequences. More than a tragic figure, Shango epitomizes the ambiguities of life. Shango "was a god who disclosed a truth about the human condition that was not easily acknowledged, but that could not be denied by the Yoruba" (Drewal, Pemberton III, and Abiodun, 159). Yoruba honor this king and *orisha* to appease his impulsive and unpredictable spirit. This staff, with multiple heads and double thunder celts, served as a dance wand through which its owner became possessed by the powerful *orisha*. A stylistically related *oshe Shango* is in the collection of the Museum für Völkerkunde in Berlin (Krieger 1978, 1:53b).

STAFF FOR ESHU/ELEGBA

(*Ogo Elegba*)
Early 20th century
Yoruba people, Nigeria
Wood and pigment
18¾ x 5¾ x 10 inches
Collection of Dr. and Mrs. Basil
    Hirschowitz

A Yoruba priest once held or wore this hooked staff over the left shoulder. In Yoruba religion the left is associated with sacredness. The figure kneeling above the staff's handle is a representation of Eshu, the Yoruba deity or *orisha* of chance and confusion. Eshu is a trickster, considered the master of the crossroads. Yoruba carvers often add an extra face, behind the elongated coiffure of a staff's main figure, to reinforce the ambiguous nature of Eshu, who is able to look in all directions at the same time. This staff's figure holds gourds—also represented on the coiffure—that serve as containers for supernatural substances. Eshu's presence warns people to act with caution and diligence so as not to fall into the traps of the trickster *orisha* (Drewal 1994, 66–67). The Yoruba deity grants favors to humans if properly honored but will create trouble and despair if angered (Drewal, Pemberton III, and Abiodun 1989, 28–29).

LIDDED CONTAINER FOR DIVINATION IMPLEMENTS

(*Opon igede Ifa*)
Master Arowogun (1880–1954)
Yoruba people, Nigeria, Osi Ilorin, Ekiti
Wood and pigment
23 x 17 x 17 inches
Collection of Mary E. Cumming

This carved wooden vessel served as a container for implements used by a *babalawo*, a Yoruba diviner or priest of Ifa. Through divine or spiritual means, diviners find cause of and resolution to the problems of their clients. This container presents a series of scenes that articulate a Yoruba world order while "evoking, invoking, and activating diverse [cosmological] forces;" an arrangement that symbolizes the Yoruba concept of the universe as "one of continuous change and transformation" (Drewal, Pemberton III, and Abiodun 1989, 16–19). The four decorated open-work bands that crown the bowl—associated with the cardinal points—accentuate vignettes that feature a priest (holding staffs), a military figure (warrior on horse with prisoner), a mother and child, and a wealthy individual (pipe, and bicycle/technology). Figures around the lower part of the bowl seem to hold it above ground. These figures support the Yoruba world or cosmos as represented in the upper register. Low-relief wood carvings in this bowl's style have been attributed to master Arowogun or to his students. Comparable bowls attributed to Arowogun have been published by McClusky (1984, 56); Kecskési (1987, 135); Drewal, Pemberton III, and Abiodun (1989, 19); Fagaly (1989, 66–67); and Thompson (1993, 311). Door panel carvings or figures attributed to Arowogun or his students have been documented by Willett (1971, 230–31); Cole (1989, 168); Drewal, Pemberton III, and Abiodun (1989, 154); and Picton and Basani (1994, 14, 90).

MALE PERSONAL SHRINE FIGURE

(*Ikenga*)
Early 20th century
Igbo people, Nigeria
Wood, raffia, and pigment
14 x 4³/₄ x 4³/₄ inches
Collection of Mary E. Cumming

This figure represents an *ikenga*, a complex art form that embodies Igbo concepts of individuality, maleness, personal power and determination, ancestry, and the spiritual essence of life, called *chi* (Cole and Aniakor 1984, 15, 24–25). The *ikenga* is both figure and shrine, human and ancestor; and through prayers and sacrifices to the multifarious character, an individual achieves success in life. *Ikenga* figures vary in type and style from abstract rounded forms with stylized animal horns—symbol of power—to fairly naturalistic anthropomorphic figures also featuring the horned element. This finely carved *ikenga* is conceived as a stylized anthropomorphic figure smoking a pipe, with flexed legs, raised arms, and an elongated headdress. In most *ikenga* the horns are the crowning element, projecting high above the figures' heads. The individual who carved this *ikenga*, an experienced carver with a unique sense of form and design, devised the upright arms gesture to insinuate the shape of horns.

EMBLEM FOR EKPE ASSOCIATION

Early 20th century
Ejagham people, Nigeria/Cameroon
Wood, fibers, gourd, and animal skulls
54 x 44 x 12 inches
Collection of Mary E. Cumming

This reed and fiber mat, with attached animal skulls, wooden objects, and other materials, constitutes an emblem for the Ekpe association of the Ejagham. The skulls are those of animals that may have been killed and/or eaten during ceremonies for new society members (Nooter 1993, 60). A series of small animal skulls are aligned to form an **X** shape, with a round wooden drum—once covered by an animal skin—at its center. The emblem presents an obvious demarcation of space that may be symbolic in nature. The crossing lines of skulls, like the emblem itself, probably indicate the centrality of this secret association or its meeting house, stressed as a point of empowerment. The areas filled-in with other skulls and materials may relate to the space outside the association's inner sanctum, perhaps the domain of the wilderness still within the parameters of the members' influence.

RELIQUARY GUARDIAN FIGURE

(*Nlo biéri* or *eyéma biéri*)
Early 20th century
Fang people, Ngumba or Ntumu
    sub-group, Cameroon/Equatorial
    Guinea/Gabon
Wood, metal, and pigment
16 x 5 x 3 inches
Birmingham Museum of Art purchase with
    funds provided by the Traditional Arts
    Acquisition Fund; the Endowed Fund
    for Acquisitions; SONAT, Inc.; AmSouth
    Bank; and Buffalo Rock

Fang and related peoples of southern
Cameroon, Equatorial Guinea, and Gabon
create wooden sculptures (*nlo biéri* or
eyéma biéri) that serve as guardians of
their ancestors' relics. The skulls and
bones of a family's deceased illustrious
relatives are kept inside bark coffers
(*nsékh biéri*) where they remain safe under
the protection of *biéri* figures placed on
these containers (Perrois 1990, 42–43).
Ancestors provide support and protection
to their living kin in return for their
continuous prayers and offerings to the
deceased. *Biéri* serve as intermediaries
between humans and ancestors. These
figures/spiritual beings are consulted
during important undertakings such as
"hunting, fishing, travel, planting, marriage, political alliance, disagreements,
or war, etc." (Perrois, 42–43). The frontal,
formal disposition of this figure is consis-
tent with Fang stylistic conventions. The
figure has been attributed to the Ngumba,
a northern Fang sub-group/style (Elsas
1993, 222). A stylistically related *bieri*
has been attributed to the Ntumu, a
neighboring Fang sub-style (Perrois,
116–19). This figure's hairstyle may
actually represent a headdress with
decorative buttons (*nlo-o-ngo*) worn
by some Fang men and women (Perrois
1985, 138, 212).

DOUBLE-FACED MASK

(*Ngontang*)
Early 20th century
Fang people, Gabon
Wood, raffia, pigment, and kaolin
22 ¼ (with raffia) x 17 x 15 inches
Collection of Dr. and Mrs. Basil Hirschowitz

This double-faced Fang mask, called *ngontang*, represents a young white woman, a spirit that comes from the other side of the ocean from the country of white people or the world of the dead (Perrois 1979, 100). Perrois explains that Fang originally believed that Europeans were the reincarnation of their ancestral spirits who had returned from their graves. White-faced masks, with single or multiple faces, became a vehicle of adaptability to the foreign presence. A specific interpretation of *ngontang* is relative to the number of faces represented. The faces may relate to life and death, a father and a mother, or to aspects associated to the spiritual nature of Fang deities (Perrois, 101).

STANDING FEMALE FIGURE

(*Nkisi*)
Early 20th century
Bembe people, Republic of Congo
Wood, metal, hair, and pigments
11 ½ x 3 ½ x 3 inches
Collection of John B. Waterman

Bembe create *nkisi* figures to represent important ancestors and which contain the "breath" of their departed spirits (Nooter and Roberts 1993, 63). Details of the figures include intricate body scarification patterns and additive materials/ substances that may incorporate relics— nails, hairs, etc.—of deceased individuals (Felix 1995, 194). On some female figures the pubic area is charged with powerful substances to emphasize metaphorical principles related to life and regeneration (Neyt and Volavka 1988, 231–33). This Bembe female figure retains some of its original additive materials.

FEMALE NAIL FIGURE

(*Nkisi nkonde*)
Early 20th century
Vili people (?), Republic of Congo/Zaire
Wood, metal, fibers, animal skull, and
    pigments
22 x 7 x 7 inches
Birmingham Museum of Art purchase with
    funds provided by the Junior Patrons,
    the Committee for Traditional Arts, Mrs.
    Bernard S. Steiner, and Museum visitors

This "nail figure" represents a female ancestral spirit of the type called *nkisi nkonde* by Kongo, Yombe, Vili, and related peoples of the Republic of Congo, Zaire, and Angola. The nails driven into the figure signify the binding of particular contracts or associations made by two or more parties in a community with the guidance of a spiritual leader or *nganga*. People who do not honor agreements sworn before figures of this type are affected by the punitive powers of the ancestor. In rituals directed by the *nganga*, clients may summon the powers of the ancestor—through a nail— to request fertility, good health, and prosperity. The *nganga* may remove a nail from the figure after the favor requested by a client is granted by the spirit. Demvo Thomas (in MacGaffey 1991, 144) explains that the nail "wounds" anger the ancestor, who will grant a favor so that the nail or spike "comes out" ending its pain. The gland on the figure's abdomen contains an animal skull and powerful substances applied by the *nganga* to empower the figure. The large nail on the figure's back may have transformed the wooden figure into an active ancestral entity. This figure was originally attributed to the Vili, although it shows stylistic characteristics shared by other groups (Buxton 1996). Based on the study of its proportions, surface quality, and style, Marc Felix (1995, 214) has attributed this figure to the Yaa. Wyatt MacGaffey (1991, 145) published two "Mayombe" (nail) female figures with facial details that are identical to those of this figure.

ANCESTRAL MASK

Early 20th century
Yaka people, Zaire
Wood, textile, raffia, and pigment
26 x 18 x 18 inches
Collection of Dr. and Mrs. Basil Hirschowitz

Yaka masks represent ancestral spirits that protect *mukanda* male initiation camps from uninitiated individuals and other negative influences. In secluded *mukanda* camps, boys learn mores associated with adult behavior, as well as discipline, endurance, and respect for elders (Bourgeois 1993, 49). The masks guard the integrity of initiations while bringing their protective powers to their owners and their communities. Some Yaka masks are meant to look threatening, and their terrorizing performances are meant to impart obedience upon intimidated initiates. This Yaka mask incorporates a wooden face mask with an elaborate headdress constructed on a frame of cloth, twigs, and branches. Raffia is attached around the mask adding to the imposing image of the ancestral character. This mask was worn or held by an initiate and his instructor during festive ceremonies associated with graduation from *mukanda* (Bourgeoise 1984, 119–24).

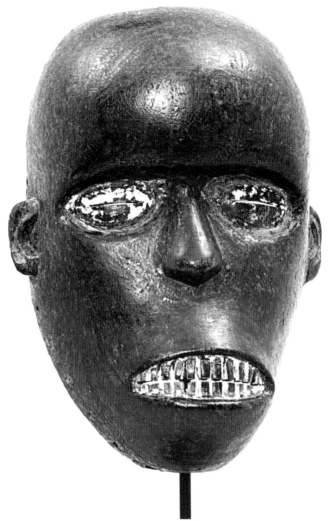

BABOON MASK

(*Hundu*)
Early 20th century
Chokwe people, Zaire/Angola
Wood and pigments
12 ½ x 5 ½ x 3 ½ inches
Collection of Dr. and Mrs. Hirschowitz

Chokwe mask performances are normally associated with the initiation of boys known as *mukanda*. These ancestors may assume human, animal, abstract, or hybrid forms as masks or *mukishi* to bring their protective spiritual influences to the initiation camp as well as to the communities hosting *mukanda* (Jordán 1993, 41–61).

This particular mask represents Hundu, the baboon (Bastin 1982, 92–93). In his performance, Hundu may carry a flywhisk and a rattle, implements that are normally associated with the power of divination. The baboon/ancestor is an ambiguous character with supernatural powers that may be directed towards the protection of the initiation camp or against individuals with evil intentions (Roberts 1995, 56–57). Some Chokwe consider baboons to be relatives of humans. The animals are said to have their own festivities during the full moon to brew their own beer and to hold their own initiations and rituals (Samukinji 1992). The reddish coloration on the surface of this mask and the blue details around the eyes are favored by Chokwe groups in Zaire.

STANDING FEMALE FIGURE

Early 20th century
Eastern/Kasai Pende people, Zaire
Wood and pigment
16 x 6 x 5 inches
Collection of Fred and Ellen Elsas

The Eastern or Kasai Pende create large male and female figures to represent royal lineage ancestors. The figures may be incorporated into the architecture of chiefs' palaces or their ritual *kibulu* houses (Strother 1993, 157–78). Eastern Pende also create large power figures that are used in divination (Robbins and Nooter 1989, 403; and Roy 1992, 136–37). Smaller-scale figurative sculptures are rare among Pende, and information about their meaning and use is scarce (Felix 1987, 140–43).

The size of this female figure and its type are uncharacteristic of architectural sculpture. The figure probably served to honor the powerful female ancestor of an important Pende family. This figure's facial features—with wavy eyebrows, downcast eyes, "high" nose, and open mouth showing filed teeth—reflect stylistic details associated with Western Pende *mbuya* masks. De Sousberghe, on the other hand, published a group of figures collected in Eastern Pende territories that are similar in style and pose to this one (1958, 144, 150; figs. 268, 269, 274). This female figure conveys a sense of dramatic presence unmatched by figures of this type.

POWER FIGURE

(*nkishi*)
Early 20th century
Songye people, Zaire
Wood, metal, animal horn,
    animal parts, shell, and gourd
18 x 6¾ x 5¾ inches
Collection of Fred and Ellen Elsas

Mankishi figures represent powerful
and auspicious Songye ancestral spirits
that protect individuals or communities
through supernatural means. Small
mankishi belong to individuals who may
privately summon their ancestors to
request favors in exchange for prayers
and offerings. Larger power figures, such
as this one, represent community *mankishi*
that are collectively owned. Large power
figures may be kept in a ritual hut, near
a chief's house, or at the center of a
village. A Songye ritual expert, or *nganga,*
normally leads negotiations with the spirit
on behalf of his community. An old man or
woman may be selected as the guardian
(*nkunja*) of an *nkishi* (singular form of
mankishi), and through his or her dreams
or in a state of spiritual possession, the
ancestor may communicate relevant
information to the community (Hersak
1985,132). Additive materials and organic
substances, called *bishimba*, include
animal horns and skins, seeds and fibers,
metal strips and tacks, wooden pegs
and miniature figures. These symbolic
and active elements or ingredients give
direction to the supernatural actions of
the *nkishi* (Hersak, 129–32).

This finely carved Songye figure still
retains an outstanding array of *bishimba*,
including several miniature *mankishi* of the
personal type. The miniature figures were
probably attached to the community figure
to reflect the personal needs of members
of a Songye community.

FEMALE MASK

(*Kifwebe*)
1900–1925
Songye people, Zaire
Wood, raffia, and pigments
16¾ x 10¼ x 8 inches
Birmingham Museum of Art purchase with funds provided by June and J. Mason Davis;
    General and Mrs. Edward M. Friend, Jr.; Fred and Ellen Elsas; the Committee for Traditional
    Arts; the Traditional Arts Acquisition Fund; and the General Acquisitions Fund

Songye create male and female wooden masks, called *bifwebe* (singular *kifwebe*), that
embody the supernatural powers of their *bwadi bwa kifwebe* secret men's society. This
mask's particular striations, flat crest, and white color are features associated with female
bifwebe. Female masks may propitiate positive supernatural forces on important ceremonial
occasions such as the death or enthronement of chiefs (Hersak 1985, 44). The whiteness of
female masks is associated with the moon and related to positive transitions and concepts
of continuity or cyclicity. Female *bifwebe* are limited to one per *bwadi* society ensemble,
whereas male masks are numerous (Hersak 1993, 150).

 This mask is a rare *kifwebe* example from the central Songye area, comparable to a mask
in the Musée Royal de l'Afrique Centrale (Tervuren, Belgium) dating to the early 1930's (Felix
1994; 1987, 164–65). This mask has a glossy surface patina, the result of continuous use and
handling in its original context. Its white pigments have turned to a light yellow color with
age.

MALE MASK

(*Kifwebe*)
Early 20th century
Songye people, Zaire
Wood and pigments
26 x 8 x 8 inches
Collection of Fred and Ellen Elsas

Whereas female *bifwebe* masks represent auspicious supernatural forces that may assist humans during significant transitions in life, their male counterparts embody the more ambiguous powers associated with the *bwadi bwa kifwebe* male secret society. Male *bifwebe* serve as regulatory agents, and their judicial powers are based on the manipulation of sorcery or *masende* (Hersak 1985, 44). Male *bifwebe* masks have high crests and broad stripes that are normally colored in red, black, and white. According to Dunja Hersak (1993, 150), male masks are categorized into hierarchical grades that reflect different degrees of mystical power. Masks with relatively low crests represent the "youth," and those with tall crests are identified as the "elder" or more experienced/powerful males. Of the three colors associated with male masks, red is the most significant. The amount of red on a mask may also relate to the magnitude of the mystical powers associated with it (Hersak 1985, 166–67; Roberts 1993, 66–72; Turner 1967, 59–92). This mask's low crest and minimal red coloration—traces of red are evident on the edges of the crest and inside its mouth—are characteristic of the male "youth" kifwebe type. The mask may symbolically suggest the potential or prospective powers of new *bwadi bwa kifwebe* members. This finely carved mask has a rich surface that combines different materials and substances that have been applied to create contrasting colors and textures.

RATTLE WITH FIGURE

Early 20th century
Hemba people, Zaire
Wood, gourds, feathers, and pigment
13¾ x 5 x 5 inches
Collection of Fred and Ellen Elsas

Luba, Hemba, Tabwa, and other related peoples of Zaire create a variety of carved wooden figures that serve as mnemonic devices, indicators of kinship ties, ancestral spirit repositories, and symbols of rank (Nooter and Roberts 1996; Roberts and Maurer 1986; Neyt 1977; Felix 1989). This Hemba figurative gourd rattle once assisted a diviner or spirit medium in summoning and sustaining the presence of a protective ancestral spirit (Nooter and Roberts, 189–91). The sinuous lines of the figure's body, part of a Hemba stylistic vocabulary, seem to stress the dynamic nature of the ancestor.

DOUBLE-FACED DIVINATION FIGURE

(*Kalunga*)
Early 20th century
Bembe people, Zaire
Wood, raffia, and pigments
2 x 1 inches
Collection of Dr. Dannetta K. Thornton Owens

This miniature double-faced figure embodies dualistic principles associated with powerful ancestral spirit forces that may assist humans if properly acknowledged. The two faces may relate to liminal or transitional states, past and future dimensions, or to the ambiguous nature of ancestors (Turner 1967, 93–111; Roberts 1986; Jordán 1996, 101–05, 120, and 1994, 17–19). According to Marc Felix (1989, 155, and 1996), this *kalunga* spirit figure may have been placed in a shrine, kept in a basket, or worn as a pendant by a Bembe dignitary. The figure's detailed facial features and expressive qualities transcend its size to impart a sense of monumental presence. The figure still retains its original red and white pigments and fiber skirt.

STAFF WITH MALE FIGURE/
STAFF WITH FEMALE FIGURE

Early 20th century
Zigua people (?), Tanzania
Wood and pigment
57 x 2 inches and 59 1/4 x 2 inches
Collection of Francois and Holly Booyse

These two staffs were collected in the early 1900s by Dr. Francois Booyse's grandfather, a British (South African) military officer who traveled extensively throughout Africa. Although figurative staffs are made by different southern African peoples (Dewey 1994, 10–13; van Wyk 1996, 90–91), these two have stylistic features that indicate they were created in Tanzania. The male figure's type of uniform and hat also support the Tanzanian attribution (van Wyk 1997). Zigua, Kwere, Luguru, Zaramo, and other neighboring peoples of Tanzania create different styles of figurative sculpture, although some pieces seem to combine elements from these diverse stylistic traditions. Because the male figure/staff is dressed in military attire, its female companion provides more clues to support a style-based attribution. Her skirt is most significant since three carved pieces by a Kwere "Master of the Skirted Lady," and others by his students, have been identified (Felix 1990, 109, 305). Compared to this figure, the Master's work is much more refined and accomplished. This figure's general form and rare "skirted" type do, however, suggest that its carver was either in contact with the Master or one his pieces. The detailed treatment of the ears on these two staffs is almost identical to that of pieces attributed to the Master carver. Although the artist who made these staffs may have been influenced by the Kwere Master, the female figure's coiffure and facial features are closer to a Zigua style of carving (Felix, 399, 412). The decorative patterns on the female figure's skirt are also found on the Zigua examples. The maker of these staffs may have worked in a workshop in Bagamoyo or Dar es Salaam where the pieces were probably collected (Felix, 109).

FUNERARY POST

(*aloalo*)
Early 20th century
Mahafaly people, Madagascar
Wood
85 x 10 x 10 inches
The Warner Collection of the Gulf States Paper
    Corporation

Mahafaly and other peoples of Madagascar carve
elaborate funerary posts to honor important
deceased individuals and to guide them in their
journey to the realm of ancestors (Sieber 1986,
30–31; Mack 1996, 71; Nooter 1989, 528). Mahafaly
grave posts, called *aloalo*, often feature an anthropomorphic figure that is surmounted by a vertical
structure of abstract designs topped by smaller
figures or figurative scenes. The bottom figures have
been interpreted as generic commemorative portraits
or as intermediaries between the world of the living
and that of the dead (Mack 1996, 71). The intercon-
nected geometric designs relate to lunar symbolism
and to the cardinal points (cross within the circle).
The figures depicted atop *aloalo* normally relate to
funerary ritual scenes. The two characters that crown
this particular grave post seem to walk together
while carrying their belongings. The figures may
represent the deceased and his/her companion in
their journey to the afterworld.

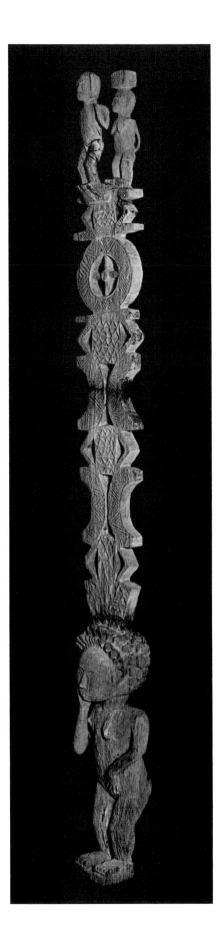

CROSS

Early 20th century
Ethiopia
Metal
12 x 5$\frac{1}{2}$ x $\frac{3}{4}$
Collection of the Wiregrass Museum of Art

DIVINER'S STAFF

(*yo domolo*)
Early 20th century
Dogon people, Mali
Wood and reptile skin
26 x 12 x 4 inches
Collection of Fred and Ellen Elsas

MEN'S SHELTER POST WITH

FEMALE FIGURE

(toguna)
Early 20th century
Dogon people, Mali
Wood
78 x 25 x 17 inches
The Warner Collection of the Gulf States
    Paper Corporation

MEN'S SHELTER POST WITH

FIGURE/MASK

(toguna)
Early 20th century
Dogon people, Mali
Wood
79¹/₂ x 19 x 12 inches
The Warner Collection of the Gulf States
    Paper Corporation

HUNTER'S SHIRT AND PANTS

Mid-20th century
Dogon people (?), Mali
Textiles, leather, horns, wood, shells, seeds, and pigment
35 x 34 inches (left), and 21 x 30 inches (right)
Collection of Robin and Carolyn Wade

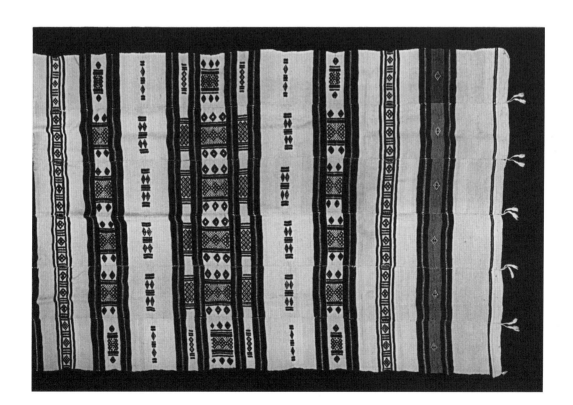

WRAPPER

1960s
Peul people, Mali
120 x 55 inches
Wool and dyes
Collection of Grady and Virginia Nunn

STANDING FEMALE DIVINATION FIGURE

Early 20th century
Senufo people, Ivory Coast
Wood, metal, and oil
9 x 3 x 2¼ inches
Collection of Fred and Ellen Elsas

GRANARY DOOR

20th century
Senufo people, Ivory Coast
Wood
54¼ x 27½ x 2 inches
Collection of the Anniston Museum of
    Natural History

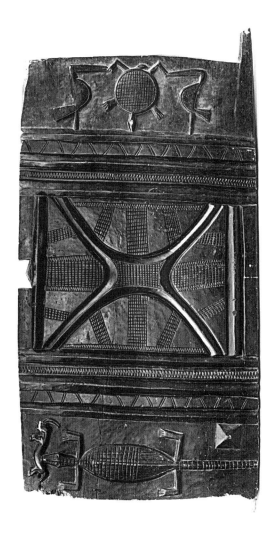

LINGUIST STAFF WITH SEATED FIGURE

Early 20th century
Akan people, Ghana
Wood and gold leaf
62 x 7 x 7 inches
Collection of Mary E. Cumming

MASK

Mid-20th century
Dan people, Liberia
Wood, metal, and hair
13 x 10 x 4 inches
Collection of FOT, Inc.

BRACELETS

Early 20th century
Yoruba people, Ogboni, Nigeria
2 are metal
5 x 3¾ inches, 5 x 3¾ inches, and 4¼ x 4 inches
Collection of Dr. and Mrs. Basil Hirschowitz

KNEELING FEMALE WITH BABY ON BACK

Early 20th century
Yoruba people, Nigeria
Ivory
5½ x 1¾ x 1¾ inches
Collection of Fred and Ellen Elsas

MOTHER AND CHILD FIGURE

Mid-20th century
Yoruba people, Nigeria
Wood and metal
12½ x 4¼ x 3½ inches
Collection of Jim Selfe

HELMET MASK

Mid-20th century
Yoruba people, Nigeria
Wood and pigments
14 1/4 x 10 x 11 1/2 inches
Collection of Dr. and Mrs. Basil Hirschowitz

BLACK-FACED ARTICULATED MASK

Early 20th century
Ibibio people, Nigeria
Wood and pigment
10 x 7 x 5 inches
Collection of Dr. and Mrs. Basil Hirschowitz

ANTHROPOMORPHIC HEADDRESS

Early 20th century
Igbo people, Nigeria
Wood, raffia, and pigment
13 x 8 1/2 x 9 inches
Collection of Dr. and Mrs. Basil Hirschowitz

WHITE-FACED ARTICULATED MASK

Early 20th century
Ogoni people, Nigeria
Wood and pigment
15 1/2 x 6 1/4 x 8 inches
Collection of Dr. and Mrs. Basil Hirschowitz

ZOOMORPHIC MASK

Early 20th century
Ejagham people, Nigeria/Cameroon
Wood, glass, and pigment
17 x 7 x 18 inches
Collection of Mary E. Cumming

HELMET MASK

Mid-20th century
Bekom people, Cameroon
Wood and pigment
23 x 9 x 12 inches
Collection of Dr. and Mrs. Basil Hirschowitz

POWER FIGURE

Early 20th century
Mambila people, Cameroon
Wood and string
11 ¼ x 5 x 5 inches
Collection of Fred and Ellen Elsas

RELIQUARY FIGURE

Early 20th century
Kota people, Gabon
Wood and metal
21 x 11 x 2 ½ inches
Collection of John B. Waterman

ANCESTRAL MASK

Early 20th century
Holo people, Zaire
Wood, raffia, and pigments
33 x 20 x 18 inches
Collection of Mary E. Cumming

DOLLS

Mid-20th century
Ndebele people, South Africa,
21½ x 7 x 9 inches, 22¾ x 7 x 6 inches, 16¼ x 7 x 5 inches, 17 x 10½ x 5 inches,
    18 x 8½ x 3 inches, 15¼ x 9 x 5 inches, and 14¾ x 7 x 4 inches
Textiles, glass beads, plastic beads, metal, wood, yarn, leather, etc.
Collection of Shia and Gaynell Hendricks

AFRICAN ART BIBLIOGRAPHY

Amick, Joan. *Art from the Forge*. Washington, D.C.: Smithsonian Institution Press, National Museum for African Art, 1995.

Bastin, Marie-Louise. *La Sculpture tshokwe*. Meudon, France: Alain et Françoise Chaffin, 1982.

Bourgeoise, Arthur P. *Art of the Yaka and the Suku*. Meudon, France: Alain et Françoise Chaffin, 1984.

———. *Face of the Spirits: Masks from the Zaire Basin*. Frank Herreman and Constantijn Petridis, eds. Antwerp: Snoeck-Ducaju and Zoon, 1993.

Buxton, John. Personal communication, 1996.

Cole, Herbert M. *Icons: Ideals of Power in the Art of Africa*. Washington, D.C.: Smithsonian Institution Press, National Museum for African Art, 1989.

Cole, Herbert M., and Chike C. Aniakor. *Igbo Arts: Community and Cosmos*. Los Angeles: U.C.L.A., Fowler Museum of Cultural History, 1984.

Dewey, William J. "Staffs from Eastern and Southern Africa." *Staffs of Life: Rods, Staffs, Scepters and Wands from the Coudron Collection of African Art*. Allen F. Roberts, ed. Iowa City: University of Iowa Museum of Art, The Project for the Advanced Study of Art and Life in Africa, 1994.

Drewal, Henry J. *Vision of Africa: The Jerome L. Joss Collection of African Art at U.C.L.A.* Doran H. Ross, ed. Los Angeles: U.C.L.A., Fowler Museum of Cultural History, 1994.

Drewal, Henry J., John Pemberton III, and Rowland Abiodun. *Yoruba: Nine Centuries of African Art and Thought*. New York: Harry N. Abrams, Inc., in association with The Center for African Art, 1989.

Elsas, Ellen. *Masterpieces East and West: From the Collection of the Birmingham Museum of Art*. Birmingham, Ala.: The Birmingham Museum of Art, 1993.

Erzini, Nadia. *Africa: The Art of a Continent*. New York: Guggenheim Museum, 1995.

Fagaly, William A. *Shapes of Power, Belief and Celebration: African Art from New Orleans Collections*. New Orleans: New Orleans Museum of Art, 1989.

Felix, Marc L. *One Hundred Peoples of Zaire and Their Sculpture*. Brussels: Tribal Arts Press, Zaire Basin Art History Research Foundation, 1987.

———. *Maniema: An Essay on the Discovery of the Symbols and Myths as Depicted in the Masks of Greater Maniema*. Munich: Verlag Fred Jahn, 1989.

———. *Mwana Hiti: Life and Art of the Matrilineal Bantu of Tanzania*. Munich: Verlag Fred Jahn, 1990.

———. As noted in the mask's certificate by the dealer, 1994.

———. *Art and Kongos: Les Peuples Kongophones et leur sculpture Biteki Bia Bakongo*. Brussels: Zaire Basin Art Research Center, 1995.

———. Personal communication, 1996.

Fischer, Eberhard, and Hans Himmelheber. *The Art of the Dan in West Africa*. Zurich: Museum Rietberg, 1984.

Galhano, Fernando. *Esculturas e objectos decorados da Guiné Portuguesa*. Lisbon: Junta de Investigações do Ultramar, 1971.

Gallois Duquette, Danielle. "Woman Power and Initiation in the Bissagos Islands." *African Arts* 12 (May 1979): 31–35.

Hersak, Dunja. *Face of the Spirits: Masks from the Zaire Basin*. Frank Herreman and Constantijn Petridis, eds. Antwerp: Snoeck-Ducaju and Zoon, 1993.

———. *Songye: Masks and Figure Sculpture*. London: TNR Productions, 1985.

Jordán, Manuel. "Le Masque comme processus ironique: Les makishi du nord-ouest de la Zambie." *Anthropologie et Sociétés*, 17:3 (1993): 41–61.

———. "Heavy Stuff and Heavy Staffs from the Chokwe and Related Peoples of Angola, Zaire, and Zambia." *Staffs of Life: Rods, Staffs, Scepters and Wands from the Coudron Collection of African Art*. Allen F. Roberts, ed. Iowa City: The Univerisity of Iowa Museum of Art, The Project for the Advanced Study of Art and Life in Africa, 1994.

———. *Tossing Life in a Basket: Art and Divination among Chokwe, Lunda, Luvale and Related Peoples of Northwestern Zambia*. Dissertation, The University of Iowa, and Michigan: University Microfilms, 1996.

Kecskési, Maria. *African Masterpieces and Selected Works from Munich: The Staatliches Museum für Völkerkunde*. New York: The Center for African Art, 1987.

Kerchache, Jacques, Jean-Louis Paudrat, and Lucien Stéphan. *L'Art Africain*. Paris: Mazenod, 1988.

Kerr, Reynold C. Personal communication, 1997.

Krieger, Kurt. *Westafrikanische Plastik*. 3 vols. Berlin: Museum für Völkerkunde, 1978.

MacGaffey, Wyatt. *Art and Healing of the Bakongo*. Bloomington: Indiana University Press, 1991.

Mack, John. *Africa: The Art of a Continent*. New York: Guggenheim Museum, 1996, 71.

Meyer, Piet. *Kunst und Religion der Lobi*. Zurich: Museum Rietberg, 1981.

McClusky, Pamela. *Praise Poems: The Katherine White Colection*. Seattle: Seattle Art Museum, 1984.

Neyt, François. *La Grande statuaire Hemba du Zaïre*. Belgium: Catholic University of Louvain, 1977.

Neyt, François, and Zdenka Volavka. *African Art from the Barbier-Mueller Colection*. Werner Schmalenbach, ed. Geneva: Prestel, 1988.

Nooter, Mary H. *Secrecy: African Art that Conceals and Reveals*. New York: The Museum for African Art, 1993.

Nooter Roberts, Mary H., and Allen F. Roberts. *Luba Art and the Making of History*. New York: The Museum for African Art, 1996.

Nooter, Nancy I. *African Art in American Collections*. Washington D.C.: Smithsonian Institution Press, 1989.

de Oliveira, Ernesto V., and Jorge Dias. *Peoples and Cultures*. Lisbon: Overseas Museum of Ethnology, 1972.

Perrois, Louis. *Arts du Gabon: Les Arts Plastiques du Bassin de l'Ogooué*. France: Arnouville, 1979.

———. *Ancestral Art of Gabon*. Geneva: Barbier-Mueller Museum, 1985.

———. *The Art of Equatorial Guinea*. New York: Rizzoli, 1990.

Picton and Basani. *The Yoruba Artist*. Rowland Abiodun, Henry J. Drewal, and John Pemberton III, eds. Washington, D.C.: Smithsonian Institution Press, 1994.

Ravenhill, Philip L. *Visions of Africa: The Jerome L. Joss Collection of African Art at U.C.L.A.* Doran H. Ross, ed. Los Angeles: U.C.L.A., Fowler Museum of Cultural History, 1994.

Robbins, Warren M., and Nancy I. Nooter. *African Art in American Collections*. Washington, D.C.: Smithsonian Institution Press, 1989.

Roberts, Allen F. "Duality in Tabwa Art." *African Arts* 19:4 (1986): 26–35.

———. "Insight, or NOT Seeing is Believing." *Secrecy: African Art that Conceals and Reveals*. Mary Nooter, ed. New York: The Museum for African Art, 1993.

———. *Animals in African Art: From the Familiar to the Marvelous*. New York: The Museum for African Art, 1995.

Roberts, Allen F., and Evan M. Maurer. *The Rising of a New Moon: A Century of Tabwa Art*. Seattle: University of Washington Press in association with the University of Michigan Museum of Art, 1986.

Roy, Christopher D. *Art and Life in Africa: Selections from the Stanley Collection*. Iowa City: The University of Iowa Museum of Art, 1992.

Samukinji, Bernard Mukuta. Personal communication, 1992.

Sieber, Roy. "A Note on History and Style." *Vigango: Commemorative Sculpture of the Mijikenda of Kenya*. Ernie Wolfe III, ed. Williamstown, Mass.: Williams College Museum of Art, 1986.

de Sousberghe, Léon. *L'Art Pende*. Brussels: Academe Royale de Belgique, 1958.

Strother, Zoe. "Eastern Pende Constructions of Secrecy." *Secrecy: African Art that Conceals and Reveals*. Mary H. Nooter, ed. New York: The Museum for African Art, 1993.

Thompson, Robert F. *Face of the Gods: Art and Altars of Africa and the African Americas*. New York: The Museum for African Art, 1993.

Turner, Victor. *The Forest of Symbols: Aspects of Ndembu Ritual*. New York: Cornell University Press, 1967.

Willet, Frank. *African Art: An Introduction*. New York: Thames and Hudson, Inc., 1971.

van Wyk, Gary. In *Africa: The Art of a Continent*. New York: Guggenheim Museum, 1996.

———. Personal communication, 1997.

NATIVE AMERICAN CULTURES

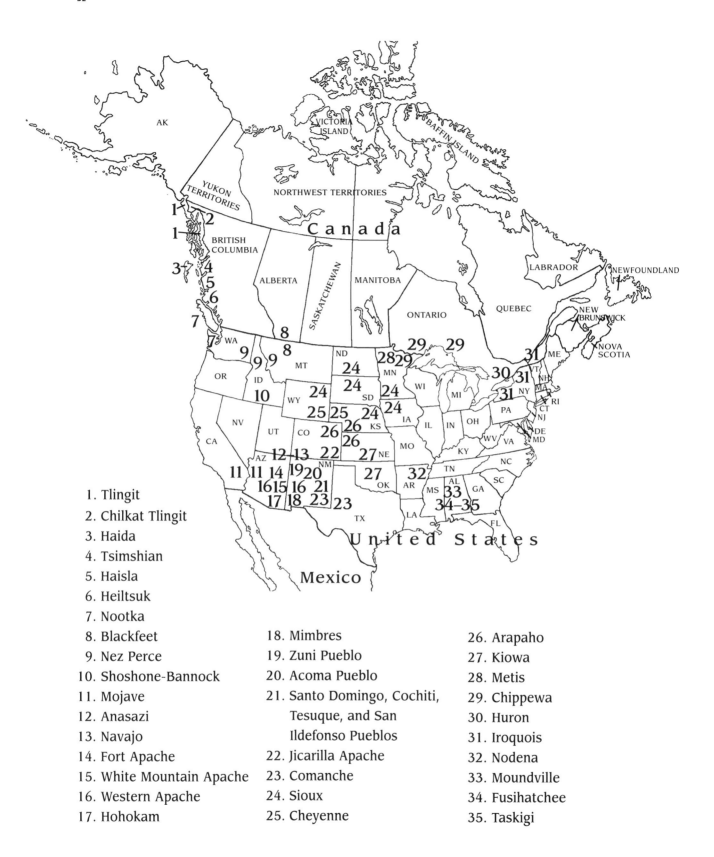

1. Tlingit
2. Chilkat Tlingit
3. Haida
4. Tsimshian
5. Haisla
6. Heiltsuk
7. Nootka
8. Blackfeet
9. Nez Perce
10. Shoshone-Bannock
11. Mojave
12. Anasazi
13. Navajo
14. Fort Apache
15. White Mountain Apache
16. Western Apache
17. Hohokam

18. Mimbres
19. Zuni Pueblo
20. Acoma Pueblo
21. Santo Domingo, Cochiti, Tesuque, and San Ildefonso Pueblos
22. Jicarilla Apache
23. Comanche
24. Sioux
25. Cheyenne

26. Arapaho
27. Kiowa
28. Metis
29. Chippewa
30. Huron
31. Iroquois
32. Nodena
33. Moundville
34. Fusihatchee
35. Taskigi

NORTH AMERICA

DANCING ROBE/BLANKET

1875–1900
Tlingit people, Chilkat style, Southeast Alaska/British Columbia
Mountain goat wool spun with yellow cedar bark, dyes
51 x 74 inches
Collection of Mary E. Cumming

Chilkat dancing robes or blankets are symbols of great prestige and wealth. They are twine-woven of mountain goat wool spun with shredded cedar bark. Women weavers use simple looms with two uprights and a cross-bar with warps free-hanging. A painted pattern board from which the blanket design is taken, showing only one side and the central elements as the blankets are always symmetrical, was created by a male artist (Samuel 1982, 45). It is difficult to determine imagery without knowing the intentions of the weaver, but this blanket has been identified as the "diving whale" type (Holm 1995).

In the late nineteenth century this type of weaving had declined, due mostly to epidemics and disruptive outside influences along the coast. Other Northwest Coast groups made the blankets, but they are collectively referred to as "Chilkat" because weavers in the remote Chilkat River Valley of southeast Alaska managed to keep the tradition alive (Dauenhauer 1995, 62).

DANCING HEADDRESS FRONTLET

1900–1925
Tlingit people, Southeastern Alaska
Wood, pigment, abalone shell, flour sack, ermine skins,
    flicker feathers, sea lion whiskers, and string
Approximately 50 x 15 x 12 inches (with trailer)
Birmingham Museum of Art purchase from the
    Rasmussen Collection

This type of dancing headdress would have been
worn with Chilkat or button blankets by persons of
high status for special occasions or performances.
Headdresses and other prestige objects were also
displayed at times when a family's history and social
stading should be recognized. The three figures carved
on this frontlet constitute the owner's family crest.
The frontlet was painted, inlaid with abalone shell,
and supported on a round frame with strips of red
woolen textile on either side. The body and trailer are
made from a commercial flour sack with ermine skin
suspensions on the sides and back. The headdress is
surmounted with a ring of red-shafted flicker feathers
and sea lion whiskers. Within that ring is a flap of
leather and some traces of swan or eagle down. During
a performance the dancer would jump lightly on his
feet and bob his head in bird-like movements. This
would cause the leather flap to fan up and down,
ejecting the down that was placed in the crown before
the dance. The down represents peace and welcome
and would float dramatically about the dancer.

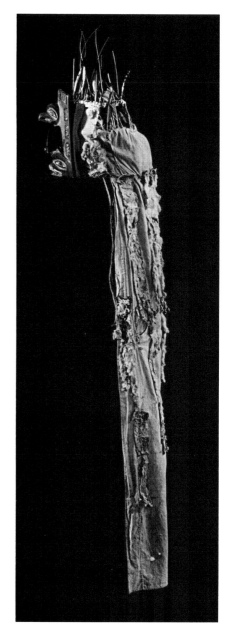

SPOON

19th century
Tlingit or Haida people, Alaska/British
  Columbia
Mountain goat horn
10 1/2 x 2 1/2 x 5 1/2 inches (on mount)
Collection of Mary E. Cumming

Small spoons of this type, made of
mountain goat horn, are sometimes
refered to as miniature totem poles,
with the family crests depicted on the
handles. The bottom figure on this
handle is a frog, whose body extends
down the back of the bowl. Above the
frog a long-snouted creature grasps its
own lower jaw. Two anthropomorphic
figures, one on the other's shoulders,
are atop the creature's head. At the top
of the handle is a small bird with curved
beak. The bowl of the spoon was cut from
the horn—steamed or boiled until soft—
and placed in a wooden mold that held
it in the desired shape until it dried and
hardened. The handles assume the
natural-curved shape of the horn and,
as in this instance, are usually carefully
pegged to the bowls.

HAT

1840–1850
Nootka people, Washington/British Columbia
Spruce root, cedar bark, and pigment
13 ½ x 12 ½ x 11 inches (on mount)
Collection of Mary E. Cumming

This bowl-shaped hat made of cedar bark and spruce root is so tightly woven it would be waterproof. Such hats apparently have a long history of use along the humid Northwest Coast. References to the wearing of twine woven hats appear in the literature after European contact in 1778, including observations by Captain Cook in 1785 (Cook 1785, 321, in Devine, 26–28). A similar hat in the Peabody Museum of Archaeology and Ethnology, Harvard University, may have been collected by Lewis and Clark between 1804 and 1806 (Wright 1991, 84–86). A virtually identical hat was depicted by Canadian artist Paul Kane being worn in Victoria, British Columbia, in 1847, and other examples have been found in archaeological sites along the Washington coast. On the hat, painted in red and black formline designs, are what may be eyes, nostrils, and a stylized mouth (Steven C. Brown). Black-rimmed hats are unique to the Nootka (Devine, 29). The rarity of black-rimmed hats in collections today suggests that the tradition must have been short-lived or confined to a small geographic area (Devine, 30).

BENTWOOD BOWL

1860–1880
Coast Tsimshian, Haisla, or Heiltsuk people, British Columbia
Yellow and red cedar and pigment
5 1/2 x 15 x 12 1/2 inches
Collection of Mary E. Cumming

The four sides of this bowl are composed of a single piece of wood. The plank, made of yellow cedar, was scored or kerfed at three corners, steamed, and bent into the rectangular form. The ends and the bottom are pegged in place. This bowl displays the characteristic bulging sides, accomplished by carving the plank before steaming. This seems to connote an overfilled vessel, perhaps reflecting its use in the potlatch where the hosts lavish gifts and vast amounts of food upon their guests (Steven C. Brown). The sides of the bowl are painted with red and black asymmetrical, formline designs. The bowl's rich patina is evidence of its being well used.

KIATUTHLANA BLACK-ON-WHITE STYLE BOWL

800–875
Anasazi culture, Cibola Province, Arizona/New Mexico
Fired clay and slip
3³/₈ x 7¹/₂ (diameter) inches
Anonymous loan

Kiatuthlana black-on-white style ceramics are considerably finer than other contemporary
Anasazi wares. Found in the area near present day Zuni Pueblo, Kiatuthlana ceramics
are very fine and thin with carefully executed designs (Peckham 1990, 65). Characteristic
of Anasazi ceramics, the design on the interior of this vessel is divided into zones with
elements shaped to fit the contour of the bowl. The Anasazi were the ancestors of the
Pueblo people, and, despite certain differences, their pottery making procedures remain
basically the same. This may to some extent be accounted for by the fact that Pueblo potters
had access to ancient Anasazi pottery and made a conscious effort to revive and maintain
ceramic traditions (Brody 1990, 7–10).

BOWL WITH COYOTE OR DOG

Classic Black-On-White, Style III, 1000–1150
Mimbres culture, New Mexico/Arizona/Mexico
Fired clay and slip
2³⁄₄ x 7³⁄₄ (diameter) inches
Collection of the Alabama Museum of Natural History, University of Alabama Museums,
  Tuscaloosa

Painted on the interior of this bowl is an animal that appears to be a coyote or a dog—the Mimbres kept domesticated dogs. In its mouth it grasps a plant with a seed head that may be maize or corn, one of the most important crops indigenous to the Americas. This is a typical example of Mimbres Black-On-White figurative pottery, with a single figure on an open, white background. Between 750 and 800, due to a change in the firing technique, the Mimbres began creating Black-On-White painted vessels (Scott 1983, 41). This ceramic tradition continued until the Mimbres culture "collapsed" around 1150. The large numbers of sherds found during the excavation of Mimbres living areas indicate that Black-On-White pottery was for everyday use; however, most complete vessels and those with figurative designs were used in a funerary context (Scott, 44).

STORAGE VESSEL

(*Olla*)
1890–1900
Zuni Pueblo, New Mexico
Fired clay and slip
9 ¼ x 12 (diameter) inches
Collection of Dick Jemison

This storage jar, or *olla,* from the late nineteenth century is in the Zuni Polychrome style, with black and red designs painted on a white-slipped background. The hatched images on the sides may be highly stylized birds. The vessel's appealing, irregular shape results from its having been hand formed; the pottery wheel was not traditionally used in the Americas. Early accounts indicate that Zuni women used ground prehistoric pottery shards as a source for temper (Batkin 1987, 164).

The coming of the railroad to the Southwest in the 1880s boosted the tourist trade, and many beautiful, large vessels from that period can be found in museums and private collections. However, the quality of Zuni pottery deteriorated around the turn of the century, largely due to the same tourist market's demands for garish "curiosities" such as ceramic moccasins (Batkin 165).

DOUGH BOWL

1910–1920
Santo Domingo Pueblo, New Mexico
Fired clay and slip
9¼ x 17 (diameter) inches
Birmingham Museum of Art purchase in memory of James A. Villadsen with funds provided
    by family and friends, the docents and staff of the Birmingham Museum of Art, the
    Committee for the Traditional Arts, Martha Villadsen Wright, Mississippi Materials
    Company, Dunn Investment Company, and Orbital Sciences Corporation.

Pueblo women first began to make dough bowls after Spanish contact and the introduction
of wheat into their diet. The large, deep vessels were necessary for the mixing, kneading, and
rising of dough in the production of leavened bread (Batkin 1987, 23). The red-slipped under-
body band of this bowl indicates that it may have been made at the Santo Domingo Pueblo,
where this design characteristic became popular shortly after the turn of the century (Batkin,
100; Snow 1994).

DOUBLE SADDLE BLANKETS

1900–1940
Navajo people, Four Corners area, Southwest region
Sheep wool and aniline and vegetal dyes
48 1/2 x 31 inches and 53 1/2 x 31 inches
Collection of John B. Waterman

The Navajo began weaving double saddle blankets in the early nineteenth century. Women wove them for the men in their families and for trade to ranchers and cowboys (Baer 1996, 44). The blankets served their purpose so well that they became an integral part of cowboys' gear throughout the American West (Amsden 1972, 103). Women sometimes wove strands of their hair or threads from clothing into blankets woven for family as insurance that the blanket and its owner would always return (Baer, 44). It seems unusual that items intended for such harsh use, and that were seldom seen whole, would be so finely woven (Amsden, 104). The earliest double saddle blankets were twill-woven, a technique borrowed from the Pueblo and adapted for use by the Navajo (Hedlund 1987, 32–33). The twill weave provided a much softer, thicker blanket (Amsden, 104).

It is not uncommon to see double saddle blankets woven asymmetrically, with different patterns or colors on each side, as they were folded in half when in use (Amsden, 104). The centers of double saddle blankets were often left blank because the decorative edges are all that show when under a saddle. They were referred to by traders as "windows," "ghost rugs," or "blanks" (Baer, 42, 44).

BURDEN OR HARVEST BASKET

Mid-20th century
Western Apache people, possibly Fort Apache, Arizona
Mulberry, cottonwood, or willow branches with leather and dyes
20 x 16 (diameter) inches
Collection of Georgine and Jack Clarke

This classic cone-shaped burden or harvest basket is twine-woven of mulberry, cottonwood, or willow branches with three encircling bands of checkerboard decoration. The bottom is overlaid with leather, and bands of leather with decorative fringe extend from rim to base. The Apache were originally a nomadic people and are recognized for the development of the fine basketry necessary to that life-style— portable and not easily broken. Such baskets traditionally served as gift or food containers in ceremonies such as a young girl's coming-of-age, although their ceremonial use had diminished in recent years (Guy 1977, 15; Coe 1977, 208). They were also used by Apache women to gather and carry edible foods (Turnbaugh and Turnbaugh 1986, 225). Burden baskets were traditionally carried on the back, supported by a tumpline extending across the wearer's forehead (Ferg 1987, 75).

PAIR OF DOLLS

1900–1920
Southern Athapascan, Jicarilla Apache people, Northeastern New Mexico/Colorado
Female, 17 x 7 x 3 inches; male, 18 x 4 x 3 inches
Leather, textiles, hair, yarn, string, glass beads, and pigment
Collection of George and June Ritchey

The Jicarilla Apache are closely related to the Navajo and other Athapascan-speaking groups of the Southwest. However, they resided on the periphery of the Plains, and the influence of groups from that region can be seen in their dress. These two dolls are dressed in the pre-Reservation style. Jicarilla Apache men wore their hair in two braids and dressed in buckskin shirts, leggings, and moccasins of the Plains style. Women's dress was also of buckskin, reaching to below the knees with a cape or poncho over the shoulders. The women also wore braids, bootlike moccasins, and wide leather belts (Ferg 1987, 170–72).

MAN'S FRINGED SHIRT

Collected in 1843
Upper Missouri Style, possibly Blackfeet people
Leather, porcupine quills, dyes, and pigment
57 x 52 inches
Collection of the Alabama Department of Archives and History, Montgomery

In the early nineteenth century, many artists, scientists, and naturalists, including John James Audubon, traveled up the Missouri River from St. Louis to explore the North American interior. At forts along the way they were able to trade with the local Native Americans. This shirt and a quilled European-style coat (p. 66) were collected by Edward Harris, an amateur botanist who in 1843 traveled with Audubon on the upper Missouri to Fort Union, located on the present-day border of Montana and North Dakota. Due to extensive intertribal trade, marriage, and sharing of customs, and unreliable collection histories, it is often difficult or impossible to attribute these objects to any particular culture group (Penney 1992, 149). Harris' diaries indicate that Audubon's group had extensive contact with the Blackfeet (Cason 1997).

MAN'S COAT

Collected in 1843
Metis Style, eastern Dakotas
Leather, porcupine quills, dyes, and glass beads
22 ½ x 44 inches
Collection of the Alabama Department of Archives and History, Montgomery

This beautiful coat was collected by Edward Harris in the upper Missouri region in 1843. The style of this garment would indicate that it may have been created by the Metis-Sioux.

The Metis settled along the Red River in Manitoba in the early nineteenth century. They were heavily involved in the fur trade, and white influence is evident in much of their men's formal clothing. Metis women, who were often of Sioux, Cree, or Ojibwa blood, tailored military-style frock coats like this one and decorated them with exquisite designs in traditional Native American quillwork. General Custer and William "Buffalo Bill" Cody owned coats very similar to this (Penney 1992, 172–76).

FEATHERED HEADDRESS

1870-1900
Sioux people, Plains region
Leather, feathers, split buffalo or cow horn,
    porcupine quills, textiles, and dyes
Approximately 75 x 15 x 18 inches
Collection of the Birmingham Museum of Art;
    gift of Mrs. Walter F. Scott

The headpiece of this single straight-line trail headdress is lined with polka-dotted commercial cloth. It is adorned with floral quillwork designs, and a split buffalo or cow horn is mounted, one half on either side of the head.

The feathers on such headgear are of special significance. They not only represent powerful creatures of the sky, they also communicate the wearers power and aggressiveness; each may also represent a brave deed of the owner or of another member of the group. Sometimes the feathers are notched or dyed, or horse-hair plumes are attached to the ends indicating various exploits in battle (Coe 1977, 175; Hail 1980, 116; Penney 1992, 215; Vestal 1957, 94). The fact that the feathers on this headdress are grouped in alternating sections, dyed and undyed, may have a particular meaning (Hail, 119). Long, trailing headdresses were intended to be worn while on horseback. A leather thong, here missing, was often attached to the end of the trailer and was used to lift and prevent the end from dragging on the ground when the wearer was on foot (Hail, 118).

PAIR OF MAN'S BURIAL MOCCASINS WITH BEADED SOLES

Late 19th/early 20th century
Oglala Sioux people, crafted at the Oglala Boarding School of Pine Ridge, North Dakota
Leather, metal, porcupine quills, dyes, and glass beads
3½ x 4½ x 10 inches, each
Jordan Collection; courtesy of the Alabama Museum of Natural History, University of Alabama
    Museums, Tuscaloosa

Plains women first began decorating the soles of moccasins around 1890. Most fully-beaded articles date to the late-nineteenth-century reservation period. Although apparently impractical, the fact that such moccasins were actually worn is illustrated in period photographs and by the presence of soil and the broken beads on the soles (Hail 1980, 111).

The colors of this pair of moccasins are unusual, and some of the beads used are very old. They may have been taken from an older, worn object reused. Reconstructing or reusing parts of moccasins, garments, and accessories was a common practice (Baulos 1997).

CHILD'S BEADED VEST

Late 19th/early 20th century
Oglala Sioux people, crafted at the Oglala Boarding School of Pine Ridge, North Dakota
Leather, glass beads, and textiles
11 x 13 x 2 inches
Jordan Collection; courtesy of the Alabama Museum of Natural History, University of Alabama
   Museums, Tuscaloosa

This small vest was cut from native-tanned cowhide, then was sinew-sewn and fully beaded. The edges and armholes are banded with commercial textile, and leather ties close the front. The creation of Anglo garments, made of leather and then heavily beaded, began during the reservation period (post 1870) and grew to a climax in the 1890s. Boy's vests and pants sets were advertised for sale in popular journals such as *Godey's Lady's Book* in the 1870s and 1880s. Some design elements used in the beadwork may be traced to those on Caucasian rugs (Hail 1980, 79–81).

BEADED SADDLE BLANKET

Late 19th/early-20th century
Oglala Sioux people, crafted at the Oglala Boarding School of Pine Ridge, North Dakota
Leather, textiles, glass beads, and metal
76½ x 28 inches
Jordan Collection; courtesy of the Alabama Museum of Natural History, University of Alabama
  Museums, Tuscaloosa

This H-shaped saddle blanket or throw has a leather center with two slits for the girth strap, and is bordered with beaded bands. Metal bells edge each fringed end.

Two hundred years after their introduction by the Spanish, horses had spread throughout the Plains region, and by the late eighteenth century most culture groups of that region were mounted. Horses were symbols of status and wealth. Such elaborately beaded gear was generally used on special occasions and by woman riders (Hail 1980, 220).

BANDOLIER BAG

1920–1940
Chippewa people, Minnesota/Canada,
  Great Lakes region
Textiles, yarn, and glass beads
45 x 14 x ³/₄ inches
Collection of the Anniston Museum of
  Natural History

Beaded bandolier bags sometimes served utilitarian purposes but more often were displayed as symbols of wealth and status. The bags were worn over the shoulder, crossing the chest, and the wearing of more than one bag indicated a chief or person of high standing (Anderson 1986, 46–47).

The earliest beaded bandolier bags first appeared in the Great Lakes region in the second quarter of the nineteenth century (Anderson, 46). They displayed panels of loom-woven beadwork that, due to missionization and the greater availability of European goods, fell from favor around the turn of the century. This bag is typical of those produced after 1900, cut from black velvet with designs that are spot-stitched and often asymmetrical. Motifs include large flowers, vines, fruits, and sometimes non-native images such as American flags. The fringe consists of large glass beads strung on yarn and finished with tassels. Several twentieth-century bags illustrate their purely symbolic quality as they do not even have pocket openings (Anderson, 52).

Beaded bandolier bags were highly valued and extensively traded to other groups. Records indicate that a beaded bandolier bag was worth a pony among the Sioux (Gilfillan 1901, 101–02; in Anderson, 56). Plains peoples even used beaded bandoliers as horse ornamentation, placing bags around the horses' necks to hang over their chests (Hail 1987, 17; Nyholm 1994, 53).

ENGRAVED "WEEPING-EYE" MASK

Late Mississippian period, Nodena phase (1400–1650)
Nodena culture, Mississippi County, Arkansas
Shell
5 1/4 x 5 x 1 1/4 inches
Collection of the University of Alabama Museums, Office of Archaeological Services,
    Moundville

Carved shell masks are related to what is referred to in archaeology as the "Southern Cult." The "weeping-eye" designs below the eyes of this mask can be interpreted in several ways. They may refer to one of the most frequent and outstanding images in Southeastern iconography, the falcon-impersonator. This character is often depicted as a warrior figure wearing a feathered cloak. Birds were associated with the sky realm and highly revered, the falcon especially so for its aggressive hunting skills and strength. The designs may imitate falcon markings and probably represent the ritual transformation of a spirit being from the shape of a human into that of a bird (Brown 1977, 28; Penney 1985, 189). Another inhabitant of the sky realm is the Thunderbird, believed by many Native North Americans to be a giant, predatory bird whose wings produce thunder and eyes issue lightning (Penney, 180). Fire was thought to have originally been sent to earth as a thunderbolt by this celestial bird (Penney, 189). The engraved lines below the eyes may be thunderbolts.

VESSEL IN THE FORM OF A KNEELING FIGURE

Late Mississippian Period, Nodena Phase
(1400–1650)
Nodena culture, Mississippi County,
Arkansas
Fired clay and shell or sand tempering
agent
6 x 5 x 6 inches
Collection of the University of Alabama
Museums, Office of Archaeological
Services, Moundville

VESSEL IN THE FORM OF A KNEELING FIGURE

Late Mississippian Period (1550–1600)
Taskigi (site at the confluence of the Coosa
and Tallapoosa Rivers near Fort
Toulouse), Alabama
Fired clay and shell or sand tempering
agent,
8 x 5¼ x 6 inches
Collection of the Alabama Department of
Archives and History, Montgomery

The majority of these figurative vessels, excavated from many Mississippi sites in the
Southeast, are portrayed as hunchbacks with protruding spines. In many cultures such
physical deformities were indicative of special powers. Afflicted individuals have often
been the shamans, and the frequency of these depictions indicates their significance. The
mask-like, flattened facial plane of the smaller figure seems to be a design characteristic
of Mississippian Period Arkansas (Maurer 1977, 63; Hathcock 1976, 184, figs. 504–06).

ENGRAVED VESSEL

Mississippian Period, Moundville, Phase II–III (1250–1550)
Moundville culture, Moundville, Tuscaloosa County, Alabama
7 x 7 (diameter) inches
Fired clay and slip
Collection of the University of Alabama Museums, Office of Archaeological Services,
  Moundville

Moundville is situated on the Black Warrior River in Tuscaloosa and Hale counties in
west-central Alabama. Moundville was the second-largest ceremonial center in the
Southeast during the Mississippian Period, covering about 300 acres and housing an
estimated population of 3,000 at its peak between 1250 and 1550. Moundville is famous
for its fine shell-tempered pottery. The intended meaning is often obscure, but most of
the pottery is decorated with imagery relating to the Mississippian social system and
mythology (Krebs, et. al., 1986, 41–42).

SMALL VESSEL

Late Mississippian Period (1500–1680)
Fortune-Noded Style, probably traded from the lower Mississippi Valley of Mississippi, found
    at Taskigi (site at the confluence of the Coosa and Tallapoosa Rivers near Fort Toulouse),
    Alabama
Fired clay and shell or sand tempering agent
4 x 5¼ (diameter) inches
Collection of the Alabama Department of Archives and History, Montgomery

During the Mississippian Period, extensive trade routes existed throughout the Southeastern
region, focusing on the large settlements located on the banks of navigable rivers. Unworked
copper and shell, destined to be made into highly-prized elite objects, was traded from the
Great Lakes to the Gulf region. It is not unusual for objects from other regions to be found
in Mississippian archaeological excavations. This small, beautiful vessel is in the Fortune-
Noded Style, which originated in the lower Mississippi Valley in what is now Mississippi.
It was excavated at Taskigi at the confluence of the Coosa and Tallapoosa Rivers near Fort
Toulouse, Alabama (Cason 1997).

LARGE STORAGE OR CEREMONIAL VESSEL

Late Mississippian period, Alabama River phase (1550–1680)
    Coosa-Tallapoosa Valley, Alabama
Fired clay and shell or sand tempering agent
13 x 17½ (diameter) inches
Collection of the Alabama Department of Archives and History, Montgomery

Southeastern pottery was traditionally hand-formed by the coil method. Women created the pottery, which they tempered with sand or ground shell. Fossilized shells, found in deposits on river banks or from the Gulf Coast or the Great Lakes, were used in this process, or shells obtained through trade (Le Page du Pratz 1758, vol. 1, 163–64; in Swanton 1979, 550). After forming the vessel, the potter would sometimes burnish the inside surface with a small stone, making it more watertight. She decorated the upper edges of the pot by engraving with a stick or by pinching the still-soft clay at intervals between her fingers. The pot was allowed to dry, then fired by turning it upside down and building a fire around it (Swanton, 551–52). Large vessels with pointed bottoms, such as this one, would have been propped up with sticks or stones during use (Caleb Swan 1855, 692; in Swanton, 551). The shallower vessels are actually lids, displayed upside down to show their decoration. These vessels were created primarily to store grain and were sometimes secondarily used as ceremonial or burial urns (Cason 1997).

DISC-SHAPED "SHELL" OR "MOON" PENDANT

"Historic" period during fur trade (1680–1820)
Europe or Canada, used by Creek/Cherokee/Choctaw, Fusihatchee
   (site on the Tallapoosa River in Elmore County)
Silver
3³/₄ x 4 x ³/₄ inches
Collection of the Alabama Department of Archives and History, Montgomery

During the time of the fur trade, peoples of the Woodlands quickly replaced the use of copper for ornamentation with silver. Due to the great demand, many silver objects were manufactured in Europe and Canada and made available through the trade system (Hamilton 1995, 50–51). Most of the Southeastern culture groups also formed silver ornaments from European and American coins, which were pounded flat and cut into desired shapes (Swanton 1979, 495–96).

This disc pendant finds its prototype in those of the same concave shape, made of polished conch shell, that were commonly worn before European contact (Hamilton 1995, 66). Another frequently used form, the crescent or half moon gorget (see p. 88), was based on the throat-protecting bib on European helmets of the type utilized by early colonists in the Americas. The helmets were soon abandoned, but the crescent-shaped gorget continued to be worn as a badge of military rank and authority. The form was adopted by Native Americans who already viewed it as symbolic of the strength of the moon (Hamilton, 69). The Christian cross form (see p. 88) was accepted and easily adopted because it was used long before European contact, refering to the four directions, the four seasons, and the sacred fire (Hamilton, 103).

LIDDED BASKET

Early 20th century
Nootka people, Washington/British
  Columbia
Spruce root, maidenhair fern, and dyes
7 x 11 (diameter) inches
Collection of the Anniston Museum of
  Natural History

PITCHER

600–800
Early Anasazi culture, Arizona
Fired clay and slip
5 1/2 x 5 1/4 x 4 1/2 inches
Anonymous loan

GILA POLYCHROME STYLE BOWL

1250–1400
Hohokam culture, Arizona
Fired clay and slip
3 1/4 x 7 1/4 (diameter) inches
Anonymous loan

FOUR-MILE POLYCHROME STYLE
BOWL

1350–1400
Anasazi culture, Arizona
Fired clay and slip
4 x 9 (diameter) inches
Anonymous loan

STORAGE VESSEL

1890–1900
Zuni Pueblo, New Mexico
Fired clay and slip
9 x 11 (diameter) inches
Collection of Dick Jemison

STORAGE VESSEL

1890–1900
Zuni Pueblo, New Mexico
Fired clay and slip
9¾ x 11 (diameter) inches
Collection of Dick Jemison

VESSEL IN THE FORM OF A BIRD

1880–1900
Cochiti or Tesuque Pueblo, New Mexico
Fired clay and slip
6 1/2 x 7 1/2 x 6 1/2 inches
Collection of the Anniston Museum of
    Natural History

BOWL

Early 20th century
San Ildefonso Pueblo, New Mexico
Fired clay and slip
3 1/4 x 9 (diameter) inches
Collection of the Anniston Museum of
    Natural History

VESSEL

1930–1940
Acoma Pueblo, New Mexico
Fired clay and slip
6 1/2 x 7 (diameter) inches
Collection of the Anniston Museum of
    Natural History

VESSEL WITH MULTIPLE SPOUTS AND HUMAN HEAD

Early 20th century
Mojave people, California/Arizona
Fired clay and slip
7 x 5 3/4 x 5 1/2 inches
Collection of the Anniston Museum of
    Natural History

BAG

1910–1920
Western Apache or Comanche people
    Arizona/New Mexico/Texas
Leather, pigment, and glass beads
17 x 12 x ³/₄ inches
Collection of John B. Waterman

DOLL

1880–1900
White Mountain Apache people, Arizona
Leather, textiles, pea, hair, glass beads, and
    pigment
4 ¹/₂ x 3 ¹/₄ x 1 inches
Collection of George and June Ritchey

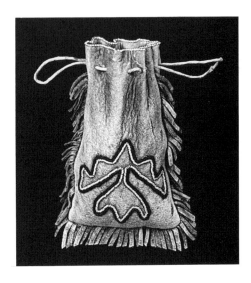

BAG

1880–1900
Possibly Kiowa people, Oklahoma
Leather, glass beads, shell, and metal
16 ¹/₂ x 3³/₄ x ³/₄ inches
Collection of John B. Waterman

BEADED DRAWSTRING BAG

Early 20th century
Nez Perce people, Idaho/Washington/
    Oregon
Leather and glass beads
7 x 6 ¹/₂ x 2 ¹/₂ inches
Collection of the Anniston Museum of
    Natural History

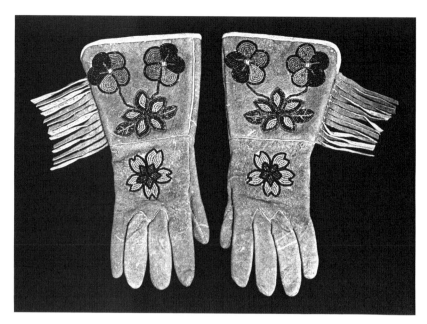

BEADED GLOVES

Late 19th/early 20th century
Shoshone-Bannock people, Idaho
Leather, textiles, and glass beads
13 x 9 inches, each
Collection of the family of Tom and Evelyn Froetscher

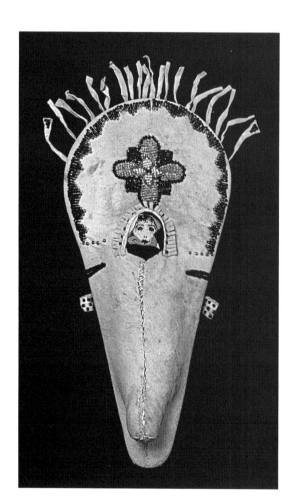

DOLL IN MINIATURE CRADLEBOARD

Late 19th/early 20th century
Shoshone-Bannock people, Idaho
Leather, textiles, glass beads, and pigment
12 x 5 1/2 x 2 inches
Collection of the family of Tom and Evelyn
  Froetscher

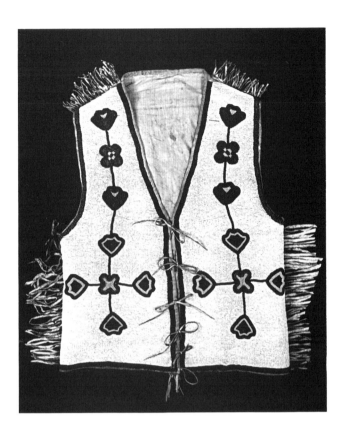

MAN'S BEADED VEST

Late 19th/early 20th century
Sioux people, Plains region
Leather, textiles, and
   glass beads
24 x 21 x 4 inches
Collection of the Anniston
   Museum of Natural History

"DISPATCH" BAG

Late 19th century
Cheyenne/Arapaho people,
   Wyoming/South Dakota/
   Nebraska/Colorado/Kansas
Leather, glass beads, and metal
$23\frac{1}{2}$ x $8\frac{1}{2}$ x $1\frac{1}{4}$ inches
Collection of the Anniston
   Museum of Natural History

PAIR OF MAN'S MOCCASINS

Late 19th/early 20th century
Cheyenne/Arapaho people, Wyoming/South
   Dakota/Nebraska/Colorado/Kansas
Leather and glass beads
5 x 4 x $11\frac{1}{2}$ inches, each
Collection of the Anniston Museum of
   Natural History

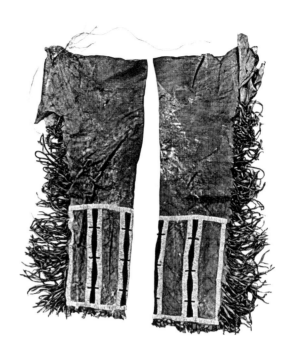

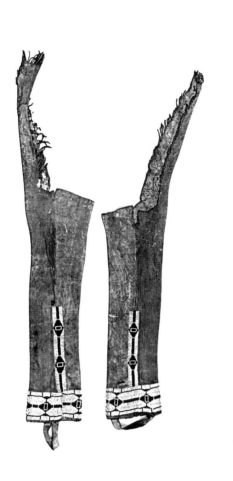

BEADED LEGGINGS

1880s
Cheyenne people, Wyoming/South Dakota/
    Nebraska
Leather, pigment, and glass beads
With blue and white beads,
    28 x 12 inches, each
Collection of the Anniston Museum of
    Natural History

BEADED LEGGINGS

1880s
Cheyenne people, Wyoming/South Dakota/
    Nebraska
Leather, pigment, and glass beads
With red, white, and blue beads,
    35 x 9 inches, each
Collection of the Anniston Museum of
    Natural History

PAIR OF MOCCASINS

Early 20th century
Huron with Iroquois beadwork on
    removable vamps, Canada/New York
Leather, textiles, and glass beads
3 1/2 x 4 1/2 x 8 1/4 inches, each
Collection of the Anniston Museum of
    Natural History

VESSEL WITH LUGS

Mississippian period,
    Moundville II-III phase, 1250–1550
Moundville culture, Moundville,
    Tuscaloosa county, Alabama
Fired clay and slip
9³/₄ x 6 (diameter) inches
Collection of the University of Alabama
    Museums, Office of Archaeological
    Services, Moundville

PAINTED VESSEL

Mississippian period,
    Moundville II-III phase, 1250–1550
Moundville culture, Moundville,
    Tuscaloosa county, Alabama
Fired clay and slip
2¹/₂ x 4 (diameter) inches
Collection of the University of Alabama
    Museums, Office of Archaeological
    Services, Moundville

STORAGE OR CEREMONIAL VESSEL LID

Late Mississippian period,
    Alabama River phase, 1550–1680
Creek, Taskigi (site at the
    confluence of the Coosa and
    Tallapoosa Rivers near Fort
    Toulouse), Alabama
Fired clay and shell or sand
    tempering agent
7³⁄₄ x 13¹⁄₂ (diameter) inches
Collection of the Alabama
    Department of Archives and
    History, Montgomery

LARGE SHALLOW STORAGE OR CEREMONIAL VESSEL LID

Late Mississippian period, Alabama River phase 1550–1680
Creek, Alabama
Fired clay and shell or sand tempering agent
5¹⁄₂ x 17 diameter
Collection of the Alabama Department of Archives and History, Montgomery

STORAGE OR CEREMONIAL VESSEL LID WITH PAINTED INTERIOR

Late Mississippian period,
    Proto-Historic, 1400–1650,
Alabama
Fired clay, shell or sand tempering
    agent, and slip
6 x 15³⁄₄ (diameter) inches
Collection of the Alabama
    Department of Archives and
    History, Montgomery

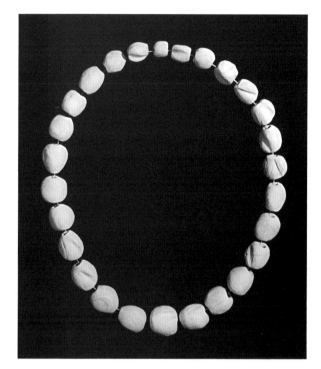

STRUNG BEADS

Archaic period, 8000–1000 B.C.
Taskigi (site at the confluence
    of the Coosa and Tallapoosa
    Rivers near Fort Toulouse), Alabama
Shell
1 inch (diameter), string of 27 beads
Collection of the Alabama Department
    of Archives and History, Montgomery

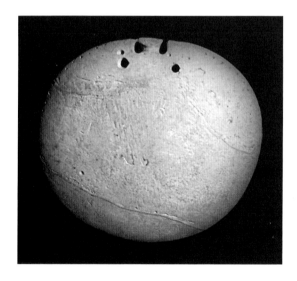

PENDANT

Archaic period 8000–1000 B.C.
Taskigi (site at the confluence of the Coosa
    and Tallapoosa Rivers near Fort
    Toulouse), Alabama
Shell
3¾ x 4 inches
Collection of the Alabama Department of
    Archives and History, Montgomery

EARSPOOLS

Archaic period 8000–1000 B.C.
Taskigi (site at the confluence of the Coosa
    and Tallapoosa Rivers near Fort
    Toulouse), Alabama
Shell
2 x 1¾ inches, each
Collection of the Alabama Department of
    Archives and History, Montgomery

CROSS

"Historic" period during fur
trade, 1680–1820
Europe or Canada, used by
Creek/Cherokee/Choctaw,
Alabama
Silver
2 1/4 x 2 1/4 inches
Collection of the Alabama
Department of Archives and
History, Montgomery

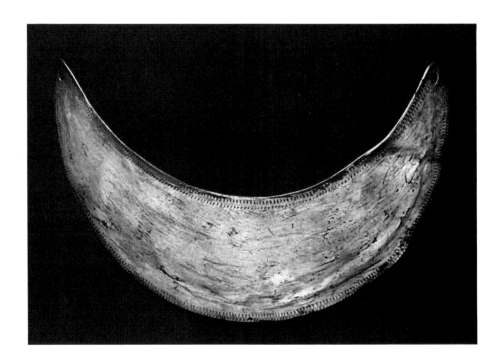

CRESCENT GORGET

"Historic" period during fur trade, 1680–1820
Europe or Canada, used by
Creek/Cherokee/Choctaw, Alabama
Silver
4 3/4 x 7 x 1 inches
Collection of the Alabama Department of
Archives and History, Montgomery

NATIVE AMERICAN ART BIBLIOGRAPHY

Amsden, Charles Avery. *Navaho Weaving: Its Technic and History*. 1934. Reprint, Glorieta, N. M.: The Rio Grande Press, 1972.

Anderson, Marcia G., and Kathy Hussey-Arntson. "Ojibwe Bandolier Bags in the Collections of the Minnesota Historical Society." *American Indian Arts Magazine* 11 (Autumn 1986): 46–57.

Baer, Joshua. "The Last Blankets." *The World of Tribal Arts*, (Summer 1996): 40–46.

Batkin, Jonathan. *Pottery of the Pueblos of New Mexico, 1700–1940*. Colorado Springs: The Taylor Museum of the Colorado Springs Fine Arts Center, 1987.

Baulos, Douglas. Personal communication, 1997

Berlant, Tony, J. J. Brody, Catherine J. Scott, and Steven A. LeBlanc. *Mimbres Pottery: Ancient Art of the American Southwest*. New York: Hudson Hills Press in association with The American Federation of Arts, 1983.

Brody, J. J. *Beauty from the Earth: Pueblo Indian Pottery from the University Museum of Archaeology and Anthropology*. Philadelphia: The University Museum of Archeaology and Anthropology, University of Pennsylvania, 1990.

Brown, James A. "Exploration into the Southeastern Image." *The Native American Heritage: A Survey of North American Indian Art*. Evan M. Maurer, ed. Chicago: Art Institute of Chicago, 1977.

Brown, Steven C. (Associate Curator, Native American, Seattle Art Museum). Personal communication with lender.

Cason, Robert. Personal communication, 1997.

Cason, Robert. Personal communication, information provided by Craig Sheldon, 1997.

Coe, Ralph T. *Sacred Circles: 2000 Years of North American Indian Art*. Kansas City: Nelson Gallery, 1977.

Dauenhauer, Nora Marks. "Tlingit At.oow: Traditions and Concepts." *The Spirit Within: Northwest Coast Native Art from the John H. Hauberg Collection*. Seattle: Seattle Art Museum, 1995.

Devine, Sue E. "Nootka Basketry Hats—Two Special Types." *American Indian Basketry Magazine*. No. 3: 26–31.

Ferg, Alan, ed. *Western Apache Material Culture: The Goodwin and Guenther Collections*. Tempe, Ariz.: The University of Arizona Press, The Arizona State Museum, 1987.

Fundaburk, Emma Lila, and Mary Douglass Fundaburk Foreman, eds. *Sun Circles and Human Hands: The Southeastern Indians Art and Industries*. Luverne, Alabama, 1957.

Guy, Hubert. "Arts and Crafts: Baskets, Beads, and Buckskin." *Arizona Highways* 53:7 (July 1977): 10–16.

Hail, Barbara A. *Hau, Kóla!: The Plains Indian Collection of the Haffenreffer Museum of Anthropology*. Providence R. I.: Brown University, 1980.

———. *Patterns of Life, Patterns of Art*. Hanover, N. H.: University Press of New England, 1987.

Hamilton, Martha Wilson. *Silver in the Fur Trade 1680--1820*. Chelmsford, Mass., 1995.

Hathcock, Roy. *Ancient Indian Pottery of the Mississippi River Valley*. Camden, 1976.

Hedlund, Ann Lane. "The Ways of the Weaver—Surviving with Style." *Well May They Be Made: Navajo Textiles from the Coleman Cooper Collection of the Birmingham Museum of Art*. Birmingham, Ala.: Birmingham Museum of Art, 1987.

Holm, Bill. Personal communication to lender, 2 February 1995.

Krebs, Phillip W., Eugene M. Futato, and Vernon James Knight, Jr. "Ten Thousand Years of Alabama Prehistory: A Pictorial Resume." *Alabama State Museum of Natural History Bulletin* 8, 1986.

Maurer, Evan M. *The Native American Heritage: a Survey of North American Indian Art.* Chicago: Art Institute of Chicago, 1977.

Nyholm, Earl. *The Proper Way.* Washington, D.C.: Smithsonian Institution Press, 1994.

Peckham, Stewart. *From This Earth: The Ancient Art of Pueblo Pottery.* Santa Fe: Museum of New Mexico Press, 1990.

Penney, David W. *Art of the American Indian Frontier: The Chandler-Pohrt Collection.* Detroit: The Detroit Institute of Arts, 1992.

Penney, David W. "Continuities of Imagery and Symbolism in the Art of the Woodlands." *Ancient Art of the American Woodland Indians.* New York: Harry N. Abrams, Inc., in association with the Detroit Institute of Arts, 1985.

Samuel, Cheryl. *The Chilkat Dancing Blanket.* Norman: University of Oklahoma Press, 1990.

Scott, Catherine J. "The Evolution of Mimbres Pottery." *Mimbres Pottery: Ancient Art of the American Southwest.* New York: Hudson Hills Press in association with The American Federation of Arts, 1983.

Snow, David H. Pueblo pottery identifications prepared for Shango Galleries, 1994.

Swanton, John R. *The Indians of the Southeastern United States.* Washington, D.C.: Smithsonian Institution Press, 1979.

Turnbaugh, Sarah Peabody and William A. *Indian Baskets.* West Chester, Penn.: Schiffer Publications, Ltd., 1986.

Vestal, Stanley. *Sitting Bull: Champion of the Sioux.* Norman: University of Oklahoma Press, 1957.

Wright, Robin K., ed. *A Time of Gathering: Native Heritage in Washington State.* Seattle: University of Washington Press in association with the Burke Memorial Washington State Museum, 1991.

PRECOLUMBIAN CULTURES

1. Colima
2. Maya
3. Veracruz
4. Olmec
5. Teotihuacan
6. Aztec
7. Coclé
8. Vicús
9. Moche
10. Huari
11. Inca

CENTRAL AND SOUTH AMERICA

SEATED SHAMAN

100 B.C.–A.D. 300
Colima culture, west Mexico
Fired clay and slip
16 1/2 x 14 1/2 x 8 inches
Collection of Charlotte and Brent Springford

The Colima, Jalisco, and Nayarit cultures of ancient west Mexico produced a variety of ceramic figures and figurative vessels, found in the context of shaft-and-chamber tombs (von Winning 1974). This type of tomb and figurative ceramic style is not found among other Mesoamerican cultures. The meaning and symbolic associations attributed to these figures continue to be the subject of scholarly debate (Kan, Meighan, and Nicholson 1989; Furst 1985). This hollow ceramic figure may be interpreted as a warrior or a shaman. The figure's particular headdress, pendant, and posture have been associated with those of shamans or warriors. The figure's gesture, with raised arms and a closed fist, is described as a protective action against sinister supernatural forces—that come from the left side—to threaten the deceased (Furst 1965, 29–80; 1978, 32–33).

SEATED MALE

100 B.C.--A.D. 300
Colima culture, west Mexico
Fired clay and slip
21 x 10 x 8 inches
Collection of Charlotte and Brent
    Springford

The various forms, actions, and gestures
of Colima shaft-and-chamber tomb figures
provide clues about their probable func-
tions as guardians or guides of the souls
of deceased individuals (Furst 1978, 26–77).
Whereas shamanistic figures may serve
to protect the deceased from negative
influences, other types of figures seem to
illustrate ritual practices that may have
ensured the transition of the soul from
this life to the next. This seated figure
holds a bowl while sitting on a stool.
The miniature bowl probably represents a
container for trance-inducing substances
used to engage in transit between the
realm of the living and that of the dead.
In other examples, the figure—possibly
a shaman—seems to drink from the bowl
(Kan, Meighan, and Nicholson 1989, 135;
Furst 1978, 37, 67; von Winning 1974, 104).
This finely modeled figure still retains most
of its original coloration. A piece almost
identical to this one, probably made by
the same artist, is published under the
"Pihuamo style" classification (von
Winning, 178).

CERAMIC MASK

100 B.C.–A.D. 300
Colima culture, west Mexico
Fired clay and slip
8¾ x 7½ x 3 inches
Collection of Charlotte and Brent Springford

Colima ceramic masks are more enigmatic than other forms of figurative representation. The masks may relate to ambiguous principles associated with transformative events expected at the time of death. It has been suggested that masks were not worn in ritual performances, but rather used to cover the faces of the deceased (Kan, Meighan, and Nicholson 1989, 144). The occurrence of Colima human and animal (dog) figures represented as mask wearers implies that masks also may have been worn ritually (von Winning 1974, 113; Kan, Meighan, and Nicholson, 131–32, 150; Nicholson 1979, 48). This highly symbolic mask is one of the finest examples of its type. The mask's facial features are well balanced, and the forms have a tendency towards simplicity and refinement.

CYLINDER VESSEL WITH CATFISH

600–800
Maya culture, Guatemala
Fired clay and slip
7 ½ x 4 (diameter) inches
Collection of Randolph O. George

Maya created a great variety of art forms to reflect the power and prestige of rulers, account for aspects of royal ritual and every-day life, and to illustrate concepts of cosmology and world order. From pendants to architectural structures, Maya art is formally and symbolically complex. The intricacy of many of their works reflects a need to justify the exploits of an elite as well as a responsibility to maintain a sense of balance and continuity through sacrifices to their gods. The Maya world was conceptually organized in different but related levels.

The natural level was the world of humans, where people resided until death. Death marked the time for a journey through the "Underworld" (Xibalba), where ambiguous characters, demi-gods, and monsters challenged the souls through treacherous acts. The "Overworld," realm of the sky or heavens, was seen as the resting place for a few mythical characters who had outsmarted the deceiving forces of the Underworld. The Overworld represents the possibility of success and regeneration (Schele and Miller 1986). Aspects of this cyclical world order are commonly represented in Maya painted ceramics. This colorful ceramic vessel features catfish that seem to float in a single color band that probably represents river waters (Kerr 1992, 3:401). This seemingly natural scene may actually relate to the mythical story of the Hero Twins Hunahpu and Xbalanque, who, after a long ordeal in Xibalba, prepare to defeat the "Lords of Death" disguised as catfish in a river of hell (Schele and Miller, 266).

CYLINDER VESSEL WITH SEATED LORDS

600-800
Maya culture, Lowland region
Fired clay and slip
7 1/2 x 4 3/4 (diameter) inches
Collection of Randolph O. George

This polychrome vessel features two depictions of a Maya lord seated on a throne that is covered with a jaguar skin. Single figures appear in front of the lord's two representations. According to information provided by the owner of the vessel, one figure has been interpreted as God "N" coming out of a shell and communicating with the lord. The other figure wears a turtle's head as his headdress. The figure with the saurian image is associated with a specific time period called "uinal," and it resembles a glyph that indicates "birth" (Huber 1996). In another cylinder vessel, God "N" is pulled out of his shell by one of the Hero Twins who defeats him with a flint knife (Schele and Miller 1986, 288, 298).

CYLINDER VESSEL WITH FIGURES

500–900
Maya culture, Guatemala
Fired clay and slip
9 1/4 x 4 1/2 (diameter) inches
Collection of Randolph O. George

Justin and Barbara Kerr (1992) have provided interpretations of the glyphs and images represented on this vessel. According to them, the glyphs indicate "I have something to tell you. . .," and "it is dedicated. . . ." God "N" is mentioned, and the Moon Goddess, his companion, is implied. The glyphs also mention "it is his writing." It is perhaps relevant that God "N" is known as one of the patrons of writing (Schele and Miller 1986, 288). The glyphs also specify that the vessel was used for drinking cacao/chocolate. Justin and Barbara Kerr believe that these vessels serve as a form of documentation or text and not necessarily as drinking cups. The amount of information presented through this vessel's glyphs and metaphoric images support that theory. The figure holding the deer wears a deer costume with the animal's ears. The figure on the opposite side carries a trophy head while stench comes out of his body (Kerr 1992). This scene seems to occur in the Underworld, although it may represent a human reenactment of Xibalban events.

VESSEL WITH DEITY HEADS

400–900
Maya culture, Guatemala
Fired clay and slip
5 ¹⁄₂ x 4 ³⁄₄ (diameter) inches
Collection of Randolph O. George

This polychrome ceramic vessel features waterlily designs
and two skull-like anthropomorphic heads in profile. The
large eyes on the heads stress the character's rank or
importance. According to Justin and Barbara Kerr (1992),
the head and plant association indicates that this is a
representation of the Maya Waterlily God. The glyphs
also mention that it is dedicated to a specific person, and
that the vessel was used for cacao. In Justin and Barbara
Kerr's estimation, cacao or chocolate may have been
ritually offered to Maya deities. A similar God/head
representation in jade, used as a pendant and dating to
the Late Classic period (600–800), has been published by
Linda Schele and Mary Ellen Miller (1986).

TRIPOD VESSEL WITH FIGURES

Middle Classic period, 400–700
Maya culture, Lowland region, Guatemala
Fired clay and slip
6 x 5 (diameter) inches
Collection of Randolph O. George

This tripod vessel is the result of a combination of ceramic-making techniques. A dark clay was first modeled to create the bowl. The legs were made separately and then attached to the bottom of the vessel. The figurative scene was first traced on the bowl's outer wall, then carved in low relief before the firing. The vessel features a character with large eyes wearing a feathered headdress and apparently holding a warrior's shield. The head of a raptor bird and a speech scroll are depicted to his front. Astronomical references seem to direct this warrior to battle (Huber 1996). Feathered warriors are commonly depicted in Mesoamerican art (Schele and Miller 1986, 230–31, 236; Berrin and Pasztory 1993, 229).

VESSEL IN THE FORM OF A HOWLING DOG

200 B.C.–A.D. 200
Maya culture, Guatemala, Kaminaljuyú or Pacific Coast
Fired clay and slip
8 x 4½ x 11¼ inches
Collection of Randolph O. George

The Colima culture of Precolumbian West Mexico produced numerous ceramic representations of dogs. In their shaft-and-chamber tombs, these may have served as companions or guides of human souls in their journeys to the afterworld (von Winning 1974; Kan, Meighan, and Nicholson 1989; Furst 1985). This vessel in the form of a howling dog is, however, a rare animal representation from the Kaminaljuyú or Pacific Coast region Preclassic Maya (Parsons 1988, 76–77). The particular meaning and function of this figure is unknown. In other cultures howling dogs are believed to warn people of impending dangers (Roberts 1995, 31–33). The guardian animals are attributed with the ability to see things that are invisible to humans. Some black decorative patterns, that may indicate hair, are still preserved on the vessel's surface.

FIGURE OF A LORD

600–900
Maya culture, Campeche, Jaina Island
Fired clay and pigment
9 ½ x 4 x 2 inches
Anonymous loan

This ceramic figure represents a Maya lord. The figure wears characteristic symbols of rank, including the headdress, loincloth, vest, earspools, bracelets, and high-backed sandals. The lord may have originally held a weapon and a shield, also identifying the figure as that of a warrior (Schele and Miller 1986, 230–32). This naturalistic ceramic figure style is associated with the art produced on Jaina Island, off the Campeche shore of the Yucatán Peninsula. The island served as a burial ground for Late Classic Maya who interred ceramic figurines and other offerings with the deceased (Miller 1986, 156–57).

HEAD OF XIPE TOTEC

600–900
Veracruz, Mexico
Fired clay
6½ x 5½ x 5 inches
Anonymous loan

This fragment head represents Xipe Totec, also known as "our lord the flayed one." Xipe Totec is associated with ritual sacrifice, fertility, and regeneration (Miller 1986, 214). For hundreds of years, different cultures of the Gulf Coast honored the god in exchange for the fertility of their lands. To the Aztecs, Xipe Totec was the patron of gold workers and the god of springtime and renewal (Coe 1991, 552). This ceramic head portrays the deity, or its impersonator, wearing earspools and an elaborate headdress with a masquette above the forehead. The facial expression is highly dramatic, suggesting the character is in an active state of transformation.

PRIEST

600–900
Veracruz, Mexico
Fired clay
9½ x 6 x 4¼ inches
Anonymous loan

This ceramic figurine probably represents a priest or ritual impersonator of a god. The figure wears a highly elaborate costume with a goggle-eyed deity mask and a plumed headdress with an anthropomorphic head. This theatrical ensemble presents us with a view of ritual life during Precolumbian times. Priests or ritual experts were responsible for maintaining a sense of balance with numerous deities that controlled human life. The mask may be that of a storm god, or a representation of Tlaloc, the higher deity of rain and fertility (Pasztory 1992, 142). Numerous representations of Tlaloc as a goggle-eyed deity occur among different Mesoamerican cultures (Townsend 1992, 170, 172–73; Miller 1986, 75, 80).

BALLPLAYER

600–900
Veracruz, Mexico
Fired clay and slip
10 x 4 x 2 ½ inches
Anonymous loan

This ceramic figure represents a ballplayer with arm, wrist, and knee pads worn for protection from the heavy rubber ball utilized in the ballgame. The figure also wears a belt or a "yoke" used to project the ball towards ballcourt scoring zones. The Mesoamerican ballgame was sometimes played ritually to honor the gods of the Underworld in exchange for their supernatural guidance. Pre-arranged games often included captives who were sacrificed after loosing the ballgame (Schele and Miller 1986, 241–64). Ceramic figurines were often placed in graves as offerings, and some may represent ballplayers defeated by the deceased (Schele and Miller, 256).

ANTHROPOMORPHIC FIGURINE

900–600 B.C.
Olmec culture, La Venta, Mexico
Green stone and cinnabar pigment
5 3/4 x 2 1/2 x 1 inches
Anonymous loan

Figurines of this type are part of a corpus of funerary arts placed in Olmec burials as offerings (Diehl and Coe 1996, 11–25). The figurines were sometimes placed in groups suggesting scenes or specific—possibly historic—events (Tate 1996, 58; Miller 1986, 29). Olmec figures are enigmatic and purposely ambiguous. They combine adult and infant qualities and often feline characteristics. This figure's mouth is defined as that of a jaguar. These human/jaguar depictions are part of an Olmec ideology that intertwines concepts of human/royal life and fertility with visionary and regenerative supernatural powers (Coe, Diehl, et al. 1996).

LIDDED URN

400–750
Teotihuacan culture, Mexico
Fired clay and slip
28 x 16 x 13 inches
Anonymous loan

Lidded urns of this type have been found in palaces, residences, and architectural niches near the entrance of tombs in the Precolumbian city of Teotihuacan (Miller 1986, 89). Incense urns that incorporate the architectural elements of temples with a central figure or mask are called "theater type censers" (Berrin and Pasztory 1993, 216–21). Anthropomorphic heads, framed by the urns' architectural and decorative elements, represent protective Teotihuacan deities. According to Kathleen Berrin (1993, 80–81), some of the urns' decorative elements (*adornos*) may have been attached to represent prayers or favors requested from the gods. These adornments may have been removed from the urns to reflect that prayers of fertility and good fortune were answered. This particular urn may have originally displayed decorative tablets on the horizontal bands below the figurative head.

STONE HEAD OR MASK

200–750
Teotihuacan culture, central Mexico
Green stone
6 1/4 x 7 1/2 x 3 inches
The BMA Acquisition Fund, Inc.; gift of Mrs. Gay Barna in memory of her mother, Rose
  Montgomery Melhado

Teotihuacan stone heads or masks have rarely been found in an archaeological context, and their exact use is therefore unknown. It has been suggested that these may have been placed over the faces of deceased individuals as masks. Another theory supports the idea that they were actually heads for full figures with bodies constructed using perishable materials (Berrin and Pasztory 1993, 184). The eyes and mouth of this finely carved Teotihuacan head were originally decorated with shells, turquoise, and other precious materials. The additive materials must have made the mask's naturalistic forms even more realistic and expressive (Cabrera Castro 1993, 186).

QUETZALCÓATL

1200–1519
Aztec culture, central Mexico
Stone and pigment
8 x 5 x 7¾ inches
Birmingham Museum of Art purchase with funds provided by Dr. and Mrs. Keith Merrill, Jr.;
    Mr. and Mrs. F. Dixon Brooke, Jr.; the bequest of Mrs. G. F. McDonnell; Mrs. Margaret
    Steeves; Mr. and Mrs. Charles Grisham; Mr. and Mrs. Hugh Jacks; the Hess Endowed Fund;
    and the Acquisition Fund.

Quetzalcóatl was a Toltec king believed to have ruled in Tula before 986 A.D. Publicly embarrassed by a deceiver called Tezcatlipoca, the Toltec ruler left the city. When Hernando Cortés arrived at the Aztec capital of Tenochtitlan in 1519, the ruler, Motecuhzoma II, believed the conquistador was Quetzalcóatl who had returned for revenge (Miller 1986, 170–72; Pasztory 1983, 196–97). The arrival of Cortés marked the demise of the Aztec civilization. Quetzalcóatl, "the feathered serpent," had been deified and worshiped by the Aztecs. This outstanding figure represents the deified king with a human face and the body of a feathered (rattle) snake. The figure relates formally and stylistically to a larger and finer example at the Musée de l'Homme.

VESSEL WITH DEER

600–800
Coclé culture, Panama
Fired clay and slip
8 ¹/₂ x 10 (diameter) inches
Collection of Charlotte and Brent Springford

Accoding to Mary W. Helms (1992, 217–27), the cultures of ancient Panama believed in a dynamic life force found in all forms and expressions of nature. A realm of the wilderness, divided into categories, was equated with levels of human empowerment, whereas images appropriated from the wilderness may have reflected the degree of rank and supernatural abilities attributed to humans. Other images found in painted pottery and embosed metal objetcs depict humans with animal or abstract attributes that suggest a state of human transformation through supernatural means. Individuals holding this type of object/image were believed to "move between realms" (Helms 1992, 223). This jar is decorated with stylized deer figures, images that reflected the high status of its owner as an individual able to control part of a dynamic life force found in nature.

FELINE AND RODENT VESSEL

100 B.C.–A.D. 600
Vicús culture, Peru
Fired clay and slip
16 x 8 x 15 inches
Anonymous loan

This figurative ceramic vessel was created during the Florescent Period, an era of great technological and artistic advancements in Peruvian pottery (Donnan 1992, 41). The Vicús and Recuay cultures of the northern coast of Peru created vessels in the form of stylized feline creatures, as well as with other animal and human forms (Donnan, 72, 75–78). The specific meaning of these ceramic figures is not clear. This feline with a rodent on its tail may relate to a humorous "cat-and-mouse" proverbial encounter, or it may comment on the actions of mythological creatures.

STIRRUP SPOUT VESSEL WITH WINGED WARRIORS

100 B.C.–A.D. 700
Moche culture, Peru
Fired clay and slip
11 1/2 x 6 (diameter) inches
Collection of Dr. and Mrs. Charles W. Ochs

Stirrup spouted vessels are the most technologically complex of Moche ceramic container forms. The painted line drawings that normally decorate these vessels also require technical precision and expertise. Evidence suggests that "ghostlines" were used first to delineate figures before their fine outlines were actually painted with slip. These sketches secured the even distribution of figures on the surface of the vessels (Donnan 1992, 69). This stirrup spout ceramic vessel depicts the mythical battle of bird or winged warriors.

STRAP-HANDLED VESSEL WITH TWO SPOUTS

600–900
Huari culture, Peru
Fired clay and slip
5 1/2 x 4 1/2 (diameter) inches
Collection of Dr. and Mrs. Charles W. Ochs

The Huari empire developed in southern Peru from A.D. 600 to 900. Their colorful ceramics were distributed throughout other regions of that country, influencing other pottery-making traditions (Donnam 1992, 81). A characteristic of Huari ceramic decoration is that their polychrome slip-painted figures and patterns are normally outlined in black. This Huari strap-handled vessel depicts a mythical bird crouching on the ground. A very similar piece has been published by Christopher B. Donnan (1992, 82) in his book on ceramics of ancient Peru.

CUP

(Kero)
1430–1660
Inca culture, Peru
Wood, pigment, and lacquer or resin
5³⁄₄ x 5¹⁄₄ (diameter) inches
Anonymous loan

Tall wooden and ceramic cups or beakers (*kero*) were created
by different ancient Peruvian cultures and were included in their
burials as symbolic offerings (Kolata and Ponce Sangines 1992,
333; Donnan 1992, 91, 110). This Inca wooden kero has designs
and figures painted in red and yellow-ochre colors. The bottom
section of the beaker displays flowing plant motifs, whereas the
upper band integrates a figurative scene with geometric patterns.
On the upper register, a tree is flanked by two figures wearing
capes. The surrounding geometric designs seem to indicate that
the scene takes place outside an architectural setting.

TRIPOD PLATE WITH MOAN BIRD IMAGE

500–600
Maya culture, Guatemala
Fired clay and slip
3¼ x 13⅛ (diameter) inches
Collection of Randolph O. George

TRIPOD PLATE WITH MOAN BIRD IMAGE

600–900
Maya culture, Guatemala
Fired clay and slip
3¼ x 12½ (diameter) inches
Collection of Randolph O. George

FLANGED PLATE

300–600
Maya culture, Lowland
region, Guatemala
Fired clay and slip
4 x 12¾ (diameter)
inches
Collection of
Randolph O. George

CYLINDER VESSEL WITH

GLYPHS AROUND RIM

300–800
Maya culture, Guatemala
Fired clay and slip
7¼ x 4½ (diameter) inches
Collection of Randolph O. George

TRIPOD CYLINDER VESSEL WITH

MOAN BIRD IMAGES

550–950
Maya culture, Tenampua, Honduras
Fired clay and slip
5¾ x 5 (diameter) inches
Collection of Randolph O. George

SEATED DOG

600–900
Veracruz, Mexico
Fired clay and pigment
11½ x 9 x 12 inches
Anonymous loan

HEAD OF THE OLD FIRE GOD, HUEHUETEOTL

600–900
Veracruz, Mexico
Fired clay and slip
8 x 7 x 5 inches
Anonymous loan

VESSEL IN THE FORM OF A STINGRAY

850–1500
Colombia
Fired clay and slip
4 1/4 x 5 x 5 1/2 inches
Collection of
    Randolph O. George

STIRRUP VESSEL WITH CREAM-ON-RED DESIGNS

100 B.C.–A.D. 700
Moche culture, Peru
Fired clay and slip
10 3/4 x 6 (diameter) inches
Collection of Dr. and
    Mrs. Charles W. Ochs

STIRRUP-SPOUTED VESSEL WITH DOG HEAD IMAGES

100 B.C.–A.D. 700
Moche culture, Peru
Fired clay and slip
7 1/2 x 7 1/2 x 5 inches
Collection of William M. Spencer III

STRAP-HANDLED TWO-SPOUTED VESSEL WITH BIRD IMAGES

600–900
Huari culture, Peru
Fired clay and slip
6 1/2 x 7 3/4 x 5 1/2 inches
Anonymous loan

VESSEL

After 1532
Inca culture, Peru
Fired clay and European glaze
6 1/2 x 6 x 5 inches
Anonymous loan

PRECOLUMBIAN ART BIBLIOGRAPHY

Berrin, Kathleen, and Esther Pasztory. *Teotihuacan: Art from the City of the Gods*. San Francisco: The Fine Arts Museums of San Francisco, 1993.

Cabrera Castro, Rubén. In *Teotihuacan: Art from the City of the Gods*. Kathleen Berrin and Esther Pasztory, eds. San Francisco: The Fine Arts Museums of San Francisco. 1993,

Coe, Michael D. "The Aztec Empire: Realm of the Smoking Mirror." *Circa 1492: Art in the Age of Exploration*. Washington, D.C.: National Gallery of Art, 1991.

Coe, Michael D., Richard A. Diehl, et. al. *The Olmec World: Ritual and Rulership*. Princeton, N.J.: Princeton University Art Museum, 1996,

Donnan, Christopher B. *Ceramics of Ancient Peru*. Los Angeles: U.C.L.A., Fowler Museum of Cultural History, 1992.

Furst, Peter. "West Mexican Tomb Sculpture as Evidence for Shamanism in Prehispanic Mesoamerica." *Antropológica* 15 (1965): 29–80.

———. *The Ninth Level: Funerary Art from Ancient Mesoamerica*. Iowa City: The University of Iowa Museum of Art, 1978.

———. "Art for the Ancestors: Archaeology and Symbolism of West Mexican Shaft Tombs and Mortuary Sculpture." *America Before Columbus*. Nancy Kalker, ed. San Antonio: San Antonio Museum Association, 1985.

Helms, Mary W. "Cosmovision of the Chiefdoms of the Isthmus of Panama." *The Ancient Americas: Art from Sacred Landscapes*. Chicago: The Art Institute of Chicago, 1992.

Huber, Robert. In documents provided by lender, 1996.

Kan, Michael, Clement Meighan, and H. B. Nicholson. *Sculpture from Ancient West Mexico: Nayarit, Jalisco, Colima*. Los Angeles: Los Angeles County Museum of Art, 1989.

Kerr, Justin. *The Maya Vase Book: A Corpus of Rollout Photographs of Maya Vases*. Vols. 1–5. New York: Kerr Associates, 1992.

Kerr, Justin and Barbara. In documents provided by lender, 1992.

Kolata, Alan, and Carlos Ponce Sanginés. "Tiwanaku: The City at the Center." *The Ancient Americas: Art from Sacred Landscapes*. Chicago: The Art Institute of Chicago, 1992.

Miller, Mary E. *The Art of Mesoamerica from Olmec to Aztec*. London: Thames and Hudson, Inc., 1986.

Nicholson, H. B. *Pre-Columbian Art from the Land Collection*. San Francisco: California Academy of Sciences, 1979.

Parsons, Lee A., John B. Carlson, and Peter D. Joralemon. *The Face of America: The Wally and Brenda Zollman Collection of Precolumbian Art*. Indianapolis: Indianapolis Museum of Art, 1988.

Pasztory, Esther. *Aztec Art*. New York: Harry N. Abrams, Inc., 1983.

———. "The Natural World as Civic Metaphor at Teotihuacan." *The Ancient Americas: Art from Sacred Landscapes*. Chicago: The Art Institute of Chicago, 1992.

Roberts, Allen F. *Animals in African Art: From the Familiar to the Marvelous*. New York: The Museum for African Art, 1995.

Schele, Linda, and Mary E. Miller. *The Blood of Kings: Dynasty and Ritual in Maya Art*. New York: Braziller, Inc., 1986.

Tate, Carolyn E. "Art in Olmec Culture." *The Olmec World: Ritual and Rulership*. Princeton, N.J.: Princeton University Art Museum, 1996.

von Winning, Hasso. *The Shaft Tomb Figures of West Mexico*. Los Angeles: Southwest Museum, 1974.